Elizabeth I

VIP
Very Interesting People

Bite-sized biographies of Britain's most fascinating historical figures

CURRENTLY AVAILABLE

1. **William Shakespeare**	*Peter Holland*
2. **George Eliot**	*Rosemary Ashton*
3. **Charles Dickens**	*Michael Slater*
4. **Charles Darwin**	*Adrian Desmond, James Moore, and Janet Browne*
5. **Isaac Newton**	*Richard S. Westfall*
6. **Elizabeth I**	*Patrick Collinson*
7. **George III**	*John Cannon*
8. **Benjamin Disraeli**	*Jonathan Parry*
9. **Christopher Wren**	*Kerry Downes*
10. **John Ruskin**	*Robert Hewison*

FORTHCOMING

11. **James Joyce**	*Bruce Stewart*
12. **John Milton**	*Gordon Campbell*
13. **Jane Austen**	*Marilyn Butler*
14. **Henry VIII**	*E. W. Ives*
15. **Queen Victoria**	*H. C. G. Matthew and K. D. Reynolds*
16. **Winston Churchill**	*Paul Addison*
17. **Oliver Cromwell**	*John Morrill*
18. **Thomas Paine**	*Mark Philp*
19. **J. M. W. Turner**	*Luke Herrmann*
20. **William and Mary**	*Tony Claydon and W. A. Speck*

Elizabeth I

VIP
Very Interesting People

Patrick Collinson

OXFORD
UNIVERSITY PRESS

OXFORD
UNIVERSITY PRESS

Great Clarendon Street, Oxford OX2 6DP

Oxford University Press is a department of the University of Oxford.
It furthers the University's objective of excellence in research, scholarship,
and education by publishing worldwide in

Oxford New York

Auckland Cape Town Dar es Salaam Hong Kong Karachi
Kuala Lumpur Madrid Melbourne Mexico City Nairobi
New Delhi Shanghai Taipei Toronto

With offices in

Argentina Austria Brazil Chile Czech Republic France Greece
Guatemala Hungary Italy Japan Poland Portugal Singapore
South Korea Switzerland Thailand Turkey Ukraine Vietnam

Oxford is a registered trade mark of Oxford University Press
in the UK and in certain other countries

Published in the United States
by Oxford University Press Inc., New York

First published in the *Oxford Dictionary of National Biography* 2004
This paperback edition first published 2007

First published 2007

British Library Cataloguing in Publication Data

Data available

Library of Congress Cataloging in Publication Data

Data available

Typeset by SPI Publisher Services, Pondicherry, India
Printed in Great Britain
on acid-free paper by
Clays Ltd, St Ives plc

ISBN 978-0-19-953449-4

1

Contents

Preface

There is a saying in Oxford that when dining at All Souls' College the fellows come and go but the guests are always the same. It is much the same with the biography and historiography of Elizabeth I. Biographers and historians succeed each other, but the questions they address never change. Was she in truth a Virgin Queen? And, if she was, was that nearly anomalous situation her failure to marry and procreate, the consequence of gynaecological factors or of simple preference; or was it a matter of diplomatic decisions and indecisions arrived at, or evaded, in a Europe of deep confessional differences? What was Elizabeth's own religion? Above all, was Elizabeth truly Elizabeth the Great, and were the decisions which shaped the course of her reign, and helped to determine the future, her own decisions? Or were they forced upon her by what a twentieth-century prime minister called 'events, dear boy'? And insofar as we can talk of Elizabethan policy, was that policy the policy not of the monarch but of a very talented and public-spirited cluster of courtiers and counsellors? The Victorian historian J. A. Froude notoriously argued that all the achievements of the reign ought to be attributed to her minister William Cecil, Lord Burghley.

In the twentieth century, Froude's jaundiced verdict was replaced by something close to adulation, especially in the writings of Elizabeth's most reliable biographer, J. E. Neale, and of his contemporary, A. L. Rowse. More recently the pendulum has swung back the other way. Historians have begun to discuss something called 'the monarchical republic of Elizabeth I', a polity in which the queen's subjects were also citizens, freely motivated by the commitment to the commonwealth and to their religion which was often at odds with their duty of obedience to a sovereign whom they publicly celebrated, while in private shook their heads and wrung their hands; a queen, moreover, who at any moment might die and leave them on their own, obliged to fend for themselves and for their country.

This account of Elizabeth for the *Oxford Dictionary of National Biography* (2004)—for all that it was written as the quatercentenary of Elizabeth's death approached in 2003, an occasion for much queen-centred celebration in books and on the small screen—reflected this revisionist history of the reign. But revisionism may have gone too far. One of the most capable and public-spirited of Elizabeth's servants, Robert Beale, who as clerk of the privy council had daily dealings with the queen, and who understood how she could be handled, even manipulated, nevertheless advised an up-and-coming civil servant: 'You shall have to do with a princess of great wisdom, learning and experience.' No more than Beale should we underestimate those qualities. It is not a mistake made by Natalie Mears in her monograph of 2005, *Queenship and Political Discourse in Elizabethan Realms*. There was queenship as well as a multivocal political discourse. Elizabeth was not the prisoner of her privy council. That body functioned at a relatively formal level, and the queen took her advice from smaller groups, even from ones and twos, individuals who might or might not be sworn of the council. That meant she really was what Burghley once called her: the commander.

But what about that reputation for great learning? We continue to dig a little deeper into that. Without doubt Elizabeth benefited from an almost transient fashion for subjecting royal and noble women to an exacting education in ancient and modern languages and literatures, a pedagogical feature of the English Renaissance. But recent work by Aysha Pollnitz of Cambridge has found that the content of that education, for all the young Tudor royals, varied according to where they stood, from time to time, in relation to succession to the throne or to potential marriageability. And so far as Elizabeth was concerned, the depth of her exposure, especially to Greek, was exaggerated, from motives of flattery and self-promotion, by the arch-pedagogue, Roger Ascham.

Let that be emblematic of Elizabeth, woman and queen. In an age characterized by what a distinguished literary scholar has called 'self-fashioning', Elizabeth fashioned herself, but was also fashioned, and turned into a legend, by countless others, in her lifetime and long after her demise; to the extent that it will be a brave, or foolish biographer who claims to be able to present her as she really was.

Patrick Collinson
August 2006

Abbreviations

BL	British Library
CSP Ire.	H. C. Hamilton and others, eds., *Calendar of the state papers relating to Ireland*, 24 vols., National Archives (1860–1910)
CUL	Cambridge University Library
Hunt. L	Huntington Library, San Marino, California
LP Henry VIII	J. S. Brewer, J. Gairdner, and R. H. Brodie, eds., *Letters and papers, foreign and domestic, of the reign of Henry VIII*, 23 vols. in 38 (1862–1932); repr. (1965)

About the author

Patrick Collinson is Regius Professor of Modern History, Emeritus, in the University of Cambridge, and a Fellow of Trinity College. He is the author of many books and essays on the religious, social, and cultural history of Elizabethan and post-Elizabethan England.

Early life and upbringing

1

Elizabeth I (1533–1603),

queen of England and Ireland, was born between 3 and 4 o'clock on the afternoon of Sunday 7 September 1533 at Greenwich Palace, Kent, the only child of Henry VIII (1491–1547), king of England and Ireland, and his second wife, Anne (c.1500–1536), queen of England, the second of three children of Thomas Boleyn, earl of Wiltshire and earl of Ormond (1476/7–1539), courtier and nobleman, of Blickling, Norfolk, and his wife, Elizabeth (*d.* 1538).

Infancy and early childhood

Henry had married Anne in January 1533 after an untidy and protracted rupture of his first marriage to Katherine of Aragon, precipitating the constitutional and religious revolution of the Henrician reformation. On 10 September the child was baptized in the church of the Observant Franciscans at Greenwich, where her father, too, had been baptized, and named Elizabeth for her grandmother, Elizabeth (Elizabeth of York; 1466–1503). Her godfather was Thomas Cranmer, archbishop of Canterbury, who had dissolved Henry's first marriage and blessed the second. William Shakespeare and John Fletcher in *Henry VIII* later put prophetic words into Cranmer's mouth on this occasion:

> This royal infant—heaven still move about her—
> Though in her cradle, yet now promises
> Upon this land a thousand thousand blessings,
> Which time shall bring to ripeness.
> (*Henry VIII*, V.iv)

However, at the time, Elizabeth was a bitter disappointment, for it had been confidently predicted that the child would be a boy. Henry had not cast off his first wife and married a second only to acquire another daughter.

As the baptism ceremony ended, Sir Thomas Wriothesley, garter king of arms, proclaimed Elizabeth to be 'the high and mighty princess of England', which was to say, heiress presumptive to the throne, displacing her seventeen-year-old half-sister Mary (1516–1558), now deemed illegitimate. At the age of three months Elizabeth was provided with her own household, first at the royal manor of Hatfield in Hertfordshire, and then, when she was one year old, at Eltham Palace in Kent, five miles from Greenwich. Meanwhile, the household of the young woman now known only as the Lady Mary was broken up and the two sisters made to share one roof. That was not a recipe for happiness, and Mary steadfastly refused to acknowledge her baby sister as princess or to yield her precedence, although in the course of time she became reconciled to Elizabeth as a sibling, and, it seems, even grew quite fond of her. Elizabeth's earliest portraits suggest that she resembled her father in the shape of her face and her auburn hair, but had inherited her mother's coal-black eyes. Katherine died on 7 January 1536 and

Henry celebrated this happy event and took delight in showing off his little daughter Elizabeth, his good mood made all the better by the new prospect of a prince. However, before the end of the month, Anne, fourteen weeks pregnant, miscarried a son. The queen's position was now untenable, and in May she was charged with having committed adultery with no fewer than five men, one of them her own brother. On 19 May she was executed. On the following day Henry married Jane (Jane Seymour; 1508/9–1537), who died after giving birth to Edward VI (1537–1553), on 24 October 1537.

Elizabeth can have had few memories of her mother, and there was no anguished parting, since she was resident at another royal manor in Hertfordshire, Hunsdon, when Anne was arrested at Greenwich, which is hard to reconcile with the story that the queen held up her child to Henry as a last despairing gesture. There is no profit in speculating about the psychological damage which Anne's terrible end might have had on her daughter, although many of Elizabeth's biographers have found significance in the fact that she never in adult life invoked or otherwise referred to her mother. What is more certain is that in his later years Elizabeth seems to have been on good terms with her father, and to have made him her role model, although protocol required that relations remained formal, so that in her earliest surviving letter she wrote: 'heretofore I have not dared to write to him' (*Collected Works*, 5–6).

At Edward's baptism the four-year-old Elizabeth carried the christening robe (although she herself had to be carried), while Mary was godmother. Both daughters were now legally illegitimate, although this stigma was practically a fiction, as became clear in 1544 when they were restored by the Succession Act to their places as heirs to the throne. As pawns on the royal marriage chessboard they were too valuable not to be countenanced by their father. After Jane's death Edward was sent to live with his half-sisters, but mainly with Elizabeth, since Mary was at court for much of 1537 to 1547. It may be an unfounded legend that all three children shared a household presided over by Henry's sixth wife, Katherine (Katherine Parr; 1512–1548) , since there is no evidence that Elizabeth lived with Katherine before 1547.

Nurses, governesses, and early tutors

Like most members of the upper class, Elizabeth was more closely bonded to her nurses and governesses than to any of her blood relations, and it was to those old servants that she showed most loyalty. At first her 'Lady Mistress' was Lady Margaret Bryan, widow of Sir Thomas Bryan and mother of one of the king's closest companions, Sir Francis Bryan. Lady Bryan had charge in turn of the three royal infants and was clearly devoted to their welfare. A letter she wrote to Sir Thomas Cromwell in the aftermath of Anne's fall gives most of what little is known about Elizabeth's infancy: she was having painful teething problems; she was short of suitable clothes, something which her mother would not have allowed to happen, for there exist the bills accounting for Anne's heavy expenditure (£40 a month) on materials for herself and her daughter. Lady Bryan also reported that the male head of the household, Sir John Shelton, insisted that Elizabeth dine and sup in state, which was not suitable for a child of her tender age, who should not be eating fruit and drinking wine. However, Lady Bryan added: 'she is as toward a child and as gentle of conditions as ever I knew any in my life' (*LP Henry VIII*, 9.90). When Lady Bryan turned her specialist attention to the rearing of the young prince in 1537, she was replaced by Lady Blanch Herbert of

Troy, who remained head of Elizabeth's household until 1547. A lady from the west country, Katherine Champernowne, better known as Kate Astley, after her marriage to John Astley about 1545, became a member of Elizabeth's household in the 1540s. Astley had great influence with the young Elizabeth, not least over the first steps in her education, but at one point the close relationship was very nearly the undoing of them both.

The flattering memoir of Anne Boleyn composed by her chaplain, William Latimer, reports that she intended her daughter to be well trained in languages, 'that she might in after tyme be hable sufficiently to judge of all maters and embassages'. Accordingly, 'she wolde endewe her with the knowlege of all tounges, as Hebrue, Greeke, Latyne, Italian, Spanishe, Frenche' ('William Latymer's chronicklle', 63). Elizabeth, and for that matter Mary, were fortunate in being born at a time when enthusiasm for the project of educating aristocratic women was at its height, especially in Italy. In editing the works of Olympia Morata, which he later dedicated to Elizabeth, the Italian humanist and protestant Celio Secondo Curione cited no less an authority than Socrates for the opinion that women 'si diligenter instituantur' ('if they are diligently instructed') were no less 'aptas ac dociles ad literas et artes liberales' ('apt to and easily instructed in letters and liberal arts') than men (O. Morata, *Opera*, 1556, fol. A2). Among Elizabeth's contemporaries who benefited from this doctrine were Lady Jane Grey, one of only a very few people to write with affection of her tutor, John Aylmer, and whose father disapproved of all this pedagogy; and the daughters of Sir Anthony Cooke, who on the contrary vigorously promoted their education. Of these learned sisters, Mildred became the second wife of William Cecil, while Anne married Nicholas Bacon and proved herself one of the most competent translators from Latin of her generation.

Elizabeth's education began under Kate Astley. When Astley had taught her as much as she could, she acquired as tutor William Grindal, a favourite pupil of the greatest educationist of the age, Roger Ascham, who had himself been taught by John Cheke, now tutor to Edward. These young men were all products of St John's College, Cambridge, which earlier in the century John Fisher, bishop of Rochester, had established, under the patronage of Elizabeth's great-grandmother, Margaret Beaufort (1443–1509), as a leading centre of humanist erudition. It was more than a happy accident that, as queen, Elizabeth appointed as her principal secretary and leading counsellor, William Cecil, whose mind and rhetorical skills, the essence of his statesmanship, had been formed in the same school. Ascham himself kept a close eye on Elizabeth's lessons, for which he assumed direct responsibility after Grindal's untimely death in January 1548, and it is from the gossipy Ascham that most is known about her education.

By the age of ten Elizabeth was learning both Italian and French, which must mean that she was already well grounded in Latin. Her French tutor (shared with Edward) was Jean Belmaine, her Italian teacher Giovanni Battista Castiglione. Later, under Ascham's instruction, the mornings were spent in mastering Greek, both the Greek of the New Testament and more difficult authors such as Isocrates. Latin studies continued in the afternoon, with the orations of Cicero and the histories of Livy. Elizabeth's earliest surviving letter (31 July 1544) was written to Katherine Parr in somewhat convoluted Italian. Here is encountered for the first time the elegant italic hand which she was well on the way to mastering, and in which she was apparently schooled by the appropriately named Belmaine. In the full flowering of the Renaissance, fine penmanship was more than a mere technique of communication, and Elizabeth took great pride in it. However, later, as queen, her handwriting deteriorated, until she was often forced to apologize for 'these scribbled lines', her 'scribbling in haste'. She seems to have acquired some Spanish. Elizabeth was also a more than moderately accomplished musician, playing, in private, on the spinet and lute, and even composing.

A humanist education

Elizabeth would have shared the modern view that learning is a lifelong undertaking. As queen, her Greek studies with Ascham continued, and in her sixties she was still an active translator, producing her own version of Boethius's *De consolatione philosophiae*, undertaken in autumn 1593, and translations of parts of Horace's *Ars poetica* and Plutarch's *De curiositate*, in 1598. These exercises all survive, but not Elizabeth's rendering of that notoriously 'hard' author, the historian Tacitus, referred to by Henry Savile in dedicating his own translation to the queen, and by an early biographer, John Clapham. As late as 1600 she told the antiquarian William Lambarde that she was determined to be a scholar in her old age, and she spent a pleasant afternoon in the Tower of London being instructed by him in the meaning of sundry technical law terms in the ancient rolls and charters in his care.

Ascham's pedagogy was founded on the principle of double translation, both out of and back into classical and modern languages, and Elizabeth's early and precocious exercises were in this vein. Between 1545 and 1548 she regularly made translated texts her new year's gifts to her father, stepmother, and half-brother, the authors including John Calvin and the Italian reformer Bernardino Ochino. In 1545 she presented Katherine Parr with her English translation of a mystical religious poem composed by Marguerite d'Angoulême, queen of Navarre, *Miroir de l'ame pechereuse*, giving it the title *The Glasse of the Synnefull Soule*. This coincided, perhaps significantly, with thoughts of a French marriage for Elizabeth, which may have encouraged further progress in the language. The presentation copy survives in the Bodleian Library, Oxford, bound and embroidered, according to tradition, by Elizabeth herself in her favourite materials, blue velvet, silks, and silver wire. As a text the choice seems strange to modern sensibilities. Was it appropriate for an eleven-year-old to ask, even if only rhetorically: 'is there any hell so profounde that is sufficient to punish the tenth parte of my synnes?' Late in 1545 Elizabeth wrote out and bound another little book as a new year's gift for her father, her rendering into Latin, French, and Italian of Katherine Parr's own *Prayers or Meditations*, a truly prodigious achievement. In the dedicatory epistle, the only known letter of Elizabeth to Henry, she seems to anticipate her future greatness, which was hardly a realistic dream in 1545: 'May I, by this means, be indebted to you not as an imitator of your virtues but indeed as an inheritor of them' (*Collected Works*, 9–10).

When Elizabeth sent her portrait to her brother, now king (traditionally in May 1549 but more probably in 1551), she wrote: 'for the face, I grant, I might well blush to offer, but the mind I shall never be ashamed to present' (*Collected Works*, 35). How good a scholar and how good a Latinist was the mature Elizabeth? There are contemporaries who complained that their knowledge had grown rusty since their schooldays when they had been required to converse in nothing but Latin. However, this was perhaps no more than a polite convention, to which Elizabeth herself may have subscribed when in 1564 she apologized to Cambridge University for her 'barbarousness'

('I would to God you had all drunk this night of the river of Lethe, that you might forget all'), and in 1566 to Oxford University for a 'speech full of barbarisms' (ibid., 87–91). She clearly had problems with the difficult Horace, although in the case of Boethius she was not so much mistranslating as altering the sense of the text into something more regal. What became a legend in Elizabeth's own time was the impromptu Latin speech she addressed to a tactless Polish ambassador in 1597, a rhetorical *tour de force*. These were the skills which Anne coveted for her daughter: learning as an accomplishment with some practical use. But Elizabeth, unlike her cousin and successor James VI and I, was never what would now be called an intellectual, not even especially bookish, and she was not noted as a patron of learned men.

Religion

No single issue has more divided Elizabeth's historians and biographers than her religion. She has been accused, mainly by Catholics, of atheism, and praised by liberal sceptics as essentially 'politique', sharing their own pragmatic attitude to matters of faith; while protestants, in her own time and after, have celebrated her as godly Deborah, the only champion of their own true faith. She cannot have been all these things.

If the foundations of Elizabeth's learning were laid in her childhood, so it was with her religious faith. Her motto, *Semper eadem* ('Always the same'), is often understood as an indication that in these matters she never would change. It may also mean that she never had changed, not since her years with Katherine Parr. Katherine's own religious position, most fully articulated in her *The Lamentation of a Sinner* (1547), seems to have been of the kind often called 'evangelical', a religious fashion derived from the aristocratic Franco-Italianate piety of the circles in which Anne Boleyn grew up, but probably with some indebtedness to Cranmer, who as a senior privy councillor was in close attendance on Katherine as regent during her husband's absence on the Boulogne campaign of 1544. This was a religion bibliocentric, Christocentric, and well expressed in an English hymn of a later century: 'nothing in my hand I bring, simply to thy cross I cling'; but, if committed to the foundational protestant doctrine (and experience) of justification by faith alone, not disposed to pursue that doctrine into its more advanced dogmatic implications, and, as a style of piety, distinctively pre-protestant. When the protestant publicist and exile John Bale published overseas the first printed edition of Elizabeth's translation of Marguerite d'Angoulême's *Miroir*, now called *A Godly Medytacyon of the Christen Sowle*, in 1548, several subtle changes were needed to turn it into a 'godly' text in the protestant sense.

Elizabeth's parentage determined that she should be, if not some kind of protestant, no kind of Catholic, since she was the product of England's breach with Rome. As queen, and not acknowledged as such in many parts of Catholic Europe, she was bound to restore the royal supremacy which Mary had repudiated. However, her religion has been characterized as either that of an 'odd sort of Protestant' (Collinson, *Elizabethan Essays*, 114) or of 'an old sort of Protestant' (Doran, 'Elizabeth I's religion', 698). It was not the mark of a 'good' protestant to employ the rich repertory of traditional Catholic oaths with which Elizabeth frequently reinforced her speech. This was a protestant who found no difficulty in her sister's reign in conforming outwardly to the religion of the mass, which makes her one of a type denounced by Calvin as 'Nicodemite', the Nicodemism of her stepmother, which she shared, among others, with Ascham, Cecil, and her favourite churchman, the first dean of her Chapel Royal, George Carew, who was Astley's cousin. To be sure, as queen she denounced the mass, but her often professed belief in some kind of real presence in the eucharist, apparently closer to Lutheran sacramental theology than to the reformed position, seems to have been more than a mere diplomatic gesture, although on occasions it was also that. Like Katherine Parr, she venerated the symbol of the cross, which set her at odds with Elizabethan protestants who regarded it as a popish idol, and demanded that she give it the same treatment as Moses' brazen serpent, which godly King Hezekiah smashed in pieces. Instead, she set up a crucifix in her chapel and for many years resisted all attempts to have it removed. Elizabeth shared with her stepmother an old-fashioned prejudice against clerical marriage, and while it is not true that she insisted on celibacy in her bishops (most were married, some twice and one three times), it is not clear how many of those bishops were chosen by her personally rather than by their courtly patrons and her privy council.

However, what made Elizabeth a particularly odd kind of protestant was her negative attitude towards preaching, which protestants regarded as the ordinary means of salvation. Her second archbishop of Canterbury, Edmund Grindal, was scandalized when she told him that three or four preachers ought to be sufficient for a shire. The official Book of Homilies, originally envisaged as a stopgap substitute for sermons, was safer, especially since Elizabeth herself carefully vetted its contents, and so far as her own consumption of sermons was concerned, although she was bound to hear a great many, it seems to have been the ritual of the procession to and from the Chapel Royal which appealed to her more than the preaching itself.

12 Prayers rather than sermons were at the heart of Elizabeth's personal religion: prayers which were rich in devotion and humility, but also conveyed a proper sense of a hierarchy in which she related directly, and even familiarly, to God himself. Representative of this religious style is the tiny book of prayers in five languages, enriched with miniatures by Nicholas Hilliard, prepared for her use (it is not in her hand) at the time of the Alençon courtship in the late 1570s. A publication of 1569 called *Christian Prayers and Meditations* had for its frontispiece Elizabeth on her knees at prayer, the sword of justice abandoned by her side. This came to be known as 'Queen Elizabeth's prayer book', and the same image was repeated in 1578 in a further *Booke of Christian Prayers*. On this showing, and on the evidence of the religious settlement over which she presided, it may not be altogether anachronistic to call Elizabeth the true progenitor of Anglicanism.

Imperilled princess

2

The scandal of Thomas Seymour

Elizabeth's whole life was one of artificiality, and how far her religion was one of those artifices will never be known. At fourteen, however, real life caught up with her, with consequences which may have made her for ever suspicious of aspects of it. On Henry's death on 28 January 1547 Elizabeth made her household, perhaps for the first time, with Katherine Parr, now dowager queen. But about June 1547 Katherine, with indecent haste, took for her third husband the lord admiral, Thomas Seymour, Baron Seymour of Sudeley, younger brother of Edward Seymour, duke of Somerset, lord protector and governor of Edward VI. Seymour, according to undocumented legend, had only weeks before proposed marriage to Elizabeth, who knew better than to accept him. However, not for the last time, the evidence suggests that if she was averse to marriage, she was not indifferent to men like Seymour, who was handsome and made for action. There were romps in her bedchamber in which Seymour's wife was complicit, thinking it innocent fun, and on one extraordinary occasion in the garden at Hanworth, Middlesex, Katherine held Elizabeth fast while Seymour 'cut hyr gowne yn a c [100] peces' (National Archives, SP 10/6/21, fol. 55*r*).

Elizabeth was strongly attached to Seymour. John Astley warned his wife that

> the Lady Elizabeth did bere som affection to my Lord Admirall / Ffor he did mark that when eny body did talk well of my Lord Admirall / she semyd to be well pleasid therwith / & somtyme she wold blush when he were spoken of. (Hatfield, Cecil MS 150, fol. 86*r*)

Kate Astley at least pretended to be shocked, and perhaps Katherine came to see that things had gone too far, for in May 1548 Elizabeth was sent away to live with Sir Anthony Denny and his wife, who was Astley's sister, at Cheshunt, Hertfordshire—or perhaps the new arrangement was her own choice. Elizabeth was not friendless at this time. She requested assistance from Cecil during the protectorate probably because he was Somerset's secretary. In an undated letter from Astley of about 1548 she asked for his help in procuring the release of a poor man imprisoned in Scotland. Elizabeth added a postscript: 'I pray you farder this pore mans sute. Your frende, Elizabeth'. Astley noted the conventional relationship developing between her mistress and the secretary but this was strengthened by their protestantism: 'beyng so moche asured of your wellyng mynde to set forthe hyr cawses to my lord protectors grace', especially as the matter was 'so godly' (BL, Lansdowne MS 1236, fol. 41*r*–*v*).

Katherine died of puerperal fever on 5 September 1548 after giving birth, and the widower again set his sights on Elizabeth. Astley actively promoted what she now deemed to be an honourable suit, to which Elizabeth seems to have been in no way averse, although she was more cautious. However, all three, Seymour, Elizabeth, and Astley, were living dangerously. On 17 February 1549 Seymour, who was plotting against his brother in other ways, was arrested, and on 20 March he was executed for treason. Meanwhile, Astley and Thomas Parry, Elizabeth's cofferer, were clapped in the Tower and interrogated. The privy council instructed Sir Robert Tyrwhit, Katherine's former master of the horse and so possessed of an insider's knowledge, to interview Elizabeth, while Tyrwhit's wife, a distant relation of Katherine's first husband, was appointed her 'Mistress' in place of Astley. The idea was to get Elizabeth to confess to her part in what was virtually a conspiracy. However, while Astley and Parry supplied the many titillating details on which Elizabeth's biographers have feasted ever since, Elizabeth gave nothing away and stood on her royal dignity. Tyrwhit told Somerset that she was too smart to be taken in by 'policy' and commented that 'the love she sayth to Aschlay ys to be wondered at' (National Archives, SP 10/6/6, fol. 17*r*).

David Starkey has pointed out that in a later century Elizabeth would have been regarded as the victim of child abuse and a suitable case for treatment by psychologists and social workers. Other writers have suspected that in the Seymour episode are concealed the real reasons why she never married. However, the emotional world of the sixteenth century is out of modern reach, and the most that can be said is that the experience must have provided a brutal introduction to adulthood, and soon there were other lessons to be learned from events: the fall and execution of Somerset, the death of the adolescent king, the plot (his plot it seems) to put on the throne the fifteen-year-old Lady Jane Grey (which depended for its success on returning both his sisters to the status of bastards), and Mary's successful coup and triumph.

Elizabeth marked her growing up by assuming a new persona, that of a demure and respectable young woman who dressed plainly and eschewed ostentatious jewellery. Even when the dowager queen of Scotland, Mary of Guise, visited England in October 1551, provoking a frenzy of effort to adopt the latest French fashions, Elizabeth 'kepte hir olde maydenly shamefastnes' (Aylmer, sig. M4*v*). However, there is no evidence Elizabeth was at court at this time. One of her servants later remembered the day when Elizabeth walked down by the river to visit his elderly and godly mother, 'who with me and our familie joied then not a little, to heare of your godlie studie and vertuous inclination' (A. Peel, ed., *The Second Parte of a Register*, 2 vols., 1915, 2.57). Yet, by the time this cameo was recorded, the disillusioned William Fuller had decided that Elizabeth had merely been acting a part.

From December 1548 the fifteen-year-old Elizabeth was the head of her own large household, numbering between 120 and 140, based mostly in the red-brick house at Hatfield originally built by John Morton, bishop of Ely, about 1480, which she acquired from Somerset and preferred to a less comfortable Hertfordshire establishment, Ashridge. She was also a woman of property. She was assured an annual income of £3000 under her father's will and (after some difficulties which were as much political as technical, but which were easily overcome after Somerset's fall in October 1549) this was turned into a portfolio of scores of manors and houses concentrated in Buckinghamshire, Hertfordshire, Huntingdonshire, Northamptonshire, Lincolnshire, and Berkshire, but with scattered estates further afield. She was one of the greatest landowners in the kingdom, with a landed estate worth £3106 13*s*. 1*d*. per annum, and when she was under investigation in her sister's reign she said that she could not remember where all her houses were. There were indications of how Elizabeth would subsequently manage the affairs of the realm in the way that she played the Tudor equivalent of the game of Monopoly and grew ever more wealthy. After its ambitious builder's fall, Somerset Place became her town house. She did not like it, partly because it was incomplete and still a building site. However, the keeper of Somerset Place was Sir Robert Dudley, fifth son of John Dudley, duke of Northumberland. She had known him since childhood and close proximity at Somerset Place might have reinforced their relationship.

The accession of Mary and Wyatt's rebellion

Mary's accession on 19 July 1553 soon proved bad news for Elizabeth. According to information recorded by both the martyrologist John Foxe and Giacomo Soranzo, the Venetian ambassador, the queen at first insisted on Elizabeth keeping her close company, but after her coronation on 1 October kept aloof. Besides repealing all the religious legislation of Edward's reign, the first step to the reconciliation of the realm to Rome, parliament declared Henry's marriage to Katherine of Aragon valid and Mary legitimate. Mary would have liked to remove Elizabeth from her place in the succession. Despite conforming outwardly to her religion, Elizabeth's relations with her sister deteriorated rapidly. In December she left the court for Ashridge, accompanied by a retinue of almost five hundred gentlemen. She deceived no one when, halfway there, she sent a message asking Mary to send after her copes, chasubles, and other ornaments appropriate for celebrating mass.

Darker clouds began to gather as Mary made her decision to marry her Spanish cousin, Philip of Spain. It was an unpopular choice, and by late January 1554 provoked a rebellion which, if it had been more widely co-ordinated, would surely have toppled the regime, and which, confined as it was to the Kentish rising led by Sir Thomas Wyatt the younger, failed only when it reached Charing Cross and Ludgate. The inevitable executions followed swiftly, that of Lady Jane Grey and her husband, Lord Guildford Dudley, on 12 February, which was the very day that Elizabeth, suffering from a mysterious and perhaps psychosomatic illness, was removed from Ashridge and began a slow journey in a litter back to Whitehall Palace, which she reached on 23 February, the day when Henry Grey, duke of Suffolk, was beheaded. Elizabeth's prospects could hardly have been more bleak, for it was in her name that Wyatt rebelled, and she was part of the plot in so far as it had been intended to marry her to Edward Courtenay, earl of Devon, of the blood royal and last of the Yorkist line, who had been thought of as a suitable consort for Mary. Elizabeth was justifiably suspected of corresponding with the French ambassador, François Noailles, and there was further evidence of potentially treasonable approaches, although none that could be extracted from Wyatt and his accomplices that she had responded, at least, not in writing. The imperial ambassador, Simon Renard, to whose advice Mary leaned more readily than to her own privy councillors, was in no doubt that Elizabeth was too dangerous to be allowed to live, which was also the view of Stephen Gardiner, bishop of Winchester.

After three weeks in which Mary refused to see or hear from her sister, the decision was taken to commit Elizabeth to the Tower. Before boarding the barge which took her down the river on 18 March, she wrote Mary a letter which she must have hoped would save her life. She remembered hearing Somerset say that if his brother had been able to speak with him he would not have suffered, and her prayer was that 'evil persuasions' would not set one sister against the other. 'I humbly crave but only one word of answer from yourself' (*Collected Works*, 41–2).

Yet, within hours she was lodged in the very same royal apartments in the Tower from which her mother had gone out to her trial and execution.

Both before and after Wyatt's execution on 11 April, after a scaffold speech in which he exonerated Elizabeth, she was examined by the privy council, which wanted to know why she had proposed, on the eve of Wyatt's rebellion, and apparently on his advice, to move from Ashridge to the strategically placed and defensible castle of Donnington in Berkshire. The circumstances were indeed suspicious, but Elizabeth defended herself with the same sagacity which she had shown in 1549, and the will in a divided privy council to prosecute seems to have been lacking. On 19 May she was removed from the Tower to house arrest at the Oxfordshire palace of Woodstock, where her keeper was a stolid Norfolk gentleman promoted above his merits to the privy council, Sir Henry Bedingfield. The journey to Woodstock was something like a progress, for Mary was no longer popular and royals in trouble always attracted sympathy, as Mary, queen of Scots, would find twenty years later, on her regular summer jaunts from Sheffield to Buxton.

Seclusion at Woodstock

Foxe in an appendix to his *Actes and Monuments* (editions from 1563) turned these changes in fortune into an edifying story of near martyrdom, associating Elizabeth with the fate of the 300 or so protestants who were burnt at the stake by her sister's authority: 'The miraculous preservation of the Lady Elizabeth, now queen of England, from extreme calamity and danger of life'. In successive editions the story was meant to edify not least Elizabeth herself, as Foxe grew increasingly concerned about the strength of her commitment to the protestant cause.

So in 1570 what was emphasized was not so much Elizabeth's heroic endurance as 'God's providence' in preserving her, but the story was in form more like a romance than history in a modern sense, which enabled Foxe to emphasize the passivity of his heroine and what was marvellous in her preservation. She was:

> the greatest traytour in the world, clapped in the Tower, and againe tossed from thence, from house to house, from prison to prison, from post to piller, at length also prisoner in her own house, and guarded with a sort of cuttethrotes. (Foxe, 2091)

The story became a seventeenth-century legend in Thomas Heywood's play *If you Know not me you Know No Bodie, or, The Troubles of Queene Elizabeth* (in two parts and fourteen editions between 1605 and 1633).

According to Foxe, Woodstock was turned into another Tower, and Elizabeth was guarded closely day and night by as many as sixty soldiers. In truth, Woodstock was no dungeon, and Elizabeth enjoyed the company of her own people including Parry, who installed himself in town in the Bull Inn, where he did business with as many as forty visitors a day and continued to administer Elizabeth's estates, ensuring that her rents were paid and her deer not poached. Other less innocent matters may also have been discussed.

It is sometimes suggested that Elizabeth herself was Foxe's source but, if so, he would hardly have presumed to have revised her account in subsequent editions. It is more likely that Foxe depended on several informants in Elizabeth's entourage, both at the Tower and at Woodstock, including one of her women, Elizabeth Sandes, a notorious protestant who later went into exile with a group which included Lady Dorothy Stafford, who lived close to Foxe in Basel. It is probably significant that the account which Foxe compiled from these sources places in a favourable light some of Elizabeth's servants, who refused to conform to the queen's religion, while it makes no secret of the fact (perhaps intended as critical admonition) that Elizabeth herself attended mass. However, she also demanded repeatedly that she be allowed to have and read an English Bible.

Elizabeth remained at Woodstock for just under a year, twelve months during which Mary's marriage to Philip was celebrated on 25 July 1554 and consummated and a child confidently expected. Cardinal Reginald Pole arrived to complete England's reconciliation to Rome. Suddenly the obstinate Bedingfield no longer stood between Elizabeth and her sister, and she was summoned to Hampton Court to witness the birth of a prince who would make her politically irrelevant. This reconciliation was encouraged by Philip. At last she was admitted to Mary's presence at Hampton Court, and to an uneasy meeting on 21 May, intended to achieve reconciliation but in which the queen still tried to secure an admission of guilt. Events were now moving out of Mary's control. The pregnancy was false, and her husband, who now in effect deserted her, distracted by many other imperial designs, began to see in Elizabeth, now almost beyond question the heir to the throne, a means of keeping the succession out of the hands of Mary, queen of Scots. Paradoxically, Philip from now on kept Elizabeth, and her hopes of succeeding to the throne, alive.

Monarch in waiting

In October 1555 Elizabeth settled back into her old life at Hatfield, attended once more by Ascham, Parry, and Astley, but soon she was at the centre of fresh plots, the Dudley conspiracy of 1556, which once again involved the earl of Devon, and in which she may have been more actively involved than in 1554. However, it was Philip, now in Brussels, who gave explicit instructions, with which Mary complied, that Elizabeth's probable guilt should not be investigated further. As a precaution, Sir Thomas Pope, a privy councillor, was installed at Hatfield to make sure that she behaved herself and Astley was put back in the Tower.

Now the worst that could happen to Elizabeth would be marriage to some foreign prince. The candidate chosen was Philip's cousin, Emmanuel Philibert, prince of Piedmont and duke of Savoy, a diplomatic pawn squeezed between the Habsburg and Valois monarchs and from Philip's point of view a perfect consort. Elizabeth's title to succeed would be recognized, England would remain a Habsburg dependency, and Emmanuel Philibert (who was not Spanish) would be handsomely compensated for the loss of his ancestral lands. However, these calculations left out of account Elizabeth's determination not to be coerced into an unwelcome marriage by Philip's threats, which he pressed in person on his return to England in March 1557. She took advice from the French ambassador, who dissuaded her from an impulse to flee into exile. Everything would fall into her lap if she would only be patient.

Elizabeth was not all that patient and took nothing for granted. She was probably now buying support, increasing the size of the retinues which always accompanied her public appearances. As Mary's health broke down, letters were being sent to potential supporters in all parts of the country, including Sir John Thynne, who promised to hold the south-west for her, and Elizabeth was digging herself into Brocket Hall, to the north of

Hatfield. On 6 November 1558 Mary acknowledged Elizabeth as her heir, and in the days which intervened before the queen's death on 17 November Elizabeth made it clear to Philip's envoy, Gomez Suárez de Figueroa, fifth count de Feria, that she would not be beholden to Spain for her crown, which she owed to her people. It may be only with hindsight that there appears to have been a smooth transition of power. Why did Parry order a military force stationed at Berwick upon Tweed, on a hostile frontier and in wartime, to come with all convenient speed to Brocket Hall? However, Elizabeth held all the cards, and what was left of the Marian regime (Pole died within twenty-four hours of Mary) was bust. As Mary went through the process of dying, the road to Hatfield was clogged with traffic.

3 The new regime and its problems

Creating a regime

The *Annals of Queen Elizabeth* by the late Elizabethan historian Sir John Hayward opens with a dark scenario:

> Every report was greedily both inquired and received, all truthes suspected, diverse tales beleeved, many improbable conjectures hatched and nourished. Invasione of strangeres, civill dissentione, the doubtfull dispositione of the succeeding Prince, were cast in every man's conceite as present perills. (*Annals of the First Four Years of the Reign of Queen Elizabeth by Sir John Hayward*, ed. J. Bruce, CS, 7, 1840, 1)

These sentences owed as much, textually, to Tacitus and to Sir Philip Sidney's *Arcadia* as to the real circumstances of November 1558. Yet Hayward hardly exaggerated. England was still at war with France and Scotland, the treasury was exhausted, Calais lost, 'to the great dishonour of the English Nation', the queen without allies and uncomfortably dependent on her Spanish patron. So reported a better historian than Hayward, William Camden (*Historie*, trans. Norton, 14). Moreover the new queen was illegitimate, not only according to Roman law, but, until parliament ruled otherwise, by common law too.

Yet an altogether more subtle threat to Elizabeth's newly established rule was that it was represented as conditional, dependent not so much on Habsburg power as on the dispositions of her protestant subjects, and, in their perception, on the good will of God himself. John Hales, a radical survivor of the Edwardian regime, presented her 'at her first entrance to her reign' with an oration which included this warning. God, 'he only', had delivered Elizabeth from her enemies and made her queen.

> If ye fear him, and seek to do his will, then he will favour you, and preserve you to the end from all enemies, as he did king David. If ye now fall from him, or juggle with him, look for no more favour than Saul had showed to him. (Foxe, 2116–19)

It is significant that Foxe saw no occasion to put this into print until 1576.

That Elizabeth was a woman allowed, even required, such things to be said. In the ill-timed *First Blast of the Trumpet Against the Monstruous Regiment of Women* (1558), the Scottish reformer John Knox asserted that the 'imbecility' of their sex rendered women unfit to bear rule. In his riposte, ostensibly defending her title, *An Harborowe for Faithfull and Trewe Subjectes* (1559), Aylmer argued that the government of women could only be exceptional and providential, citing the precedent of the biblical figure of Deborah. He thought that there was no need for concern, since England was a mixed polity, a parliamentary monarchy, and it would not be so much government by the queen as government in her name. 'It is not she that ruleth but the laws, the executors whereof be her judges, appointed by her, her justices of the peace and such other officers' (Aylmer, sigs. II3–4r).

Elizabeth, of course, was confident that it was she who ruled, and the tension between her political ideas and those of very many of her subjects, some in the highest places, is the ground bass running through the entire history of her reign. On the very day of her accession, she is said (in a somewhat dubious source) to have warned Mary's privy councillors, who had hastily made their way to Hatfield, that she would choose for her own privy council only 'such... as in consultation I shall thinck mete, and shortlie appointe' (Harington, 2.312–14). Before she spoke, Elizabeth had appointed her old friend Cecil to be her principal secretary and the anchorman of her fledgeling government. And on 17 November Cecil was already at the desk which he would occupy for the next forty years, during the whole of which time it is often difficult to know which were his decisions and policies, which hers.

It is from Cecil's notes that it is known what was done by the first, informal, meeting of Elizabeth's privy council, which may have been gathered at Hatfield on 18 November. The privy council itself was reconstructed, excluding those who owed their positions to their personal ties with Mary and to their more than formal Catholicism. The result was a smaller and more effective privy council, with twenty former members dismissed (including all the clerics) and only ten new men admitted (none of them clerics). At the same time the royal household was reordered, with Parry knighted and made comptroller on 20 November and (the most significant of the new appointments) Dudley, once Elizabeth's fellow prisoner in the Tower, made her master of the horse. Such rapid decision making, which not all her biographers associate with Elizabeth, ran contrary to advice she had received from a political wiseacre, Sir Nicholas Throckmorton, 'to succed happilie through a discreete beginning', taking her time in making new appointments, with 'no nominacion [to] bee had or used for a time of privie councellors' (Neale, 'Sir Nicholas Throckmorton's advice', 91–8). In constructing the new regime, Elizabeth was loyal to such blood kindred as she had, promoting her Boleyn cousins, Henry Carey (1526–1596) as first Baron Hunsdon on 13 January 1559, Sir Francis Knollys (1511/12–1596) as vice-chamberlain on 14 January, and two generations of Sackvilles, the closest relations of all.

On 23 November 1558 Elizabeth rode up to London, accompanied by more than a thousand lords, ladies, and gentlemen. Her frequent moves around the city, bringing her to Whitehall for Christmas, with Mary decently buried, were public demonstrations of her popularity, so many dress rehearsals for her coronation. This took place on Sunday 15 January 1559, a date chosen as propitious on the astrological advice of the mysteriously learned Dr John Dee.

The sum of £16,000 was spent from Elizabeth's own purse on this splendid show, and an untold amount by the city. Nothing was lacking, except the bishops who, according to the *Liber regalis*, ought to have played the principal parts in the ceremony. They were either dead, too old and infirm, unacceptable to the queen, or unwilling to serve, and it was left to the very junior Owen Oglethorpe, bishop of Carlisle, to carry out the anointing with holy oils and the crowning itself. The day before, according to custom, Elizabeth processed through London from the Tower to Whitehall, carried on an open litter. According to the official panegyric which celebrated the event, London was transformed into 'a stage wherin was shewed the wonderfull spectacle of a noble hearted princesse toward her most loving people, the people's excading comfort in beholding so worthy a soveraign, and hearing so princelike a voice' (Osborn, 1559, sig. A2*v*). At intervals there were various instructive pageants, most famously a representation of Time, which prompted Elizabeth's exclamation: 'Tyme hath brought me hether' (ibid., sig. C2*v*). Parts were played and explanatory lines spoken by children, and the queen repeatedly called for the 'noise' of the many musical groups to be suspended so that their piping voices should not be drowned out.

The religious settlement

The most serious business confronting the new regime was the settlement of religion, which began in earnest when Elizabeth's first parliament opened on 25 January. The symbolism of the coronation tableaux suggested that London, at least, expected a protestant outcome; but in the early weeks of the reign there were many deliberately contradictory signals of the queen's intentions. She continued to hear mass in the Chapel Royal but distanced herself from its holiest mysteries. Whether she intended to recover the royal supremacy was concealed in her royal title by an 'etc.'. In religion at least she was as discreet as Throckmorton advised.

This discretion seems to have been abandoned when parliament met. All that is certainly known about the handling of religion in the very poorly documented 1559 parliament is that from it emerged a new Act of Supremacy (in its enacted form describing the queen as supreme governor rather than supreme head of the Church of England, which met the objections of some protestants as well as of Catholics, since only Christ was head of his church) and an Act of Uniformity imposing a Book of Common Prayer which was essentially the second Edwardian book of 1552 with a few significant alterations, again designed to reconcile confessional differences.

For centuries, historians assumed that that was what Elizabeth and her closest advisers, especially Cecil, intended from the outset. It was very much the programme recommended in a 'Device for alteration of religion', anonymous but just possibly composed by Cecil himself, which, with a decisiveness now known to have been in character, faced up to the internal and external dangers of such a policy, only to produce prevailing counter-arguments. However, in 1950, the most distinguished Elizabethan historian of his day, Sir John Neale, argued ingeniously that Elizabeth's original plan was to re-enact only the royal supremacy, leaving for a later occasion the reintroduction of protestantism. Among the factors which changed her mind was concerted resistance from a House of Commons dominated by returned exiles and other committed protestants. It was the beginning of a contention with her hotter protestant subjects which would develop as the reign progressed. However, the weight of historical opinion has subsequently swung back to where it was and it is now thought that the government got what it originally wanted, and that the only significant opposition to its policy came from Catholics, lay and clerical, in the House of Lords. To overcome that, it was necessary to stage a manipulated religious disputation at Westminster Abbey (begun on 31 March), which led to the exclusion of two bishops and a mitred abbot, with a consequential change in the voting figures in the upper house. The Act of Uniformity passed by three votes. All the bishops voted against it, two lay privy councillors, and seven other peers.

It is one thing to establish that the settlement of 1559, a very conservative settlement carried further in that direction by the extraparliamentary royal injunctions of the summer of that year, was what Elizabeth wanted, quite another to argue, as some historians have done, that there was little to choose between the queen's brand of protestantism and that of those now poised to take charge of her church, and especially the returned Marian exiles who were put up to preach at court in Lent 1559, and who were now appointed to bishoprics. Prominent among these were Edmund Grindal (London), Richard Cox (Ely), Edwin Sandys (Worcester), with the non-exile Matthew Parker (Anne Boleyn's chaplain) almost the exception to prove the rule. It cannot be assumed that these appointments were what the queen personally desired, and there is no evidence of what manoeuvres at court may have preceded the making of the settlement.

What is known is that the Nicodemite queen and her émigré bishops, who carried the torch for the martyr bishops, Cranmer, Nicholas Ridley, and Hugh Latimer, did not always see eye to eye. On her state visit to Oxford in 1566, Elizabeth endured a speech by the public orator, Thomas Kingsmill, himself the brother of an exile, in which he congratulated her for recalling from Germany the friends of Pietro Martire Vermigli (Peter Martyr) and Martin Bucer. Her responses to such effusions were normally gracious, but all she is reported to have said on this occasion was 'you would have done well had you had good matter' (Nichols, 1.209). In the convocation of 1563, which otherwise approved the Thirty-Nine Articles of Religion, it was the bishops, not 'puritans' (a word not yet invented), who did their unsuccessful best to carry through a programme of further reform, and especially to remove some of the very ceremonies which were about to divide the Elizabethan church between conformists and nonconformists. When they failed in convocation, the bishops seem to have joined in a parliamentary campaign to the same end. The price of their failure was that they were obliged to enforce policies for which many of them had no taste, so provoking an anti-episcopal reaction. The queen could not be blamed. Her bishops could, and were.

The question of marriage: first suitors

The chorus of admiring approval for Gloriana and the Virgin Queen has often obscured the serious problem posed by Elizabeth's sex. It was not only Knox who believed a female ruler to be, if not an unnatural monstrosity, an unusual and in principle undesirable exception to the regular rule governing human affairs. Apart from any other considerations, it was not clear that a woman could exercise the oldest function of a monarch, leading her forces into battle. Nor could she, in any station or walk of life, ordinarily exercise the kind of authority associated with the mental powers of a man. Women, especially widows, might manage households, but they were excluded from all public offices. Privileged women might learn languages, but they could not study the law. On one occasion Cecil was upset when a messenger discussed with the queen an ambassadorial dispatch, it 'being too much for a woman's knowledge' (Haigh, *Elizabeth I*, 9). Elizabeth was regularly visited with unsolicited male advice, often represented as the will of God, which on Pauline principles only men were authorized to interpret.

It was universally assumed that Elizabeth would marry, and for two reasons, the less pressing of which was that she should have the support of a male consort. The major and compelling reason was to secure an orderly and, if possible, male succession to the throne. So the question of her marriage, a dynastic question which had been put in many circumstances and with different suitors in mind ever since her infancy, took on a new urgency once she became queen. On 2 February 1559 a select committee of the Commons, which included all the privy councillors in the house, presented the queen with a formal request that she should marry. Elizabeth took almost a week to respond with the first of her many answers, answerless. She first declared her disposition to remain in the same 'trade of life' in which she had lived hitherto; then professed to take the petition 'in good parte', because it placed no limit on her choice; promised that if she were to marry it would not be prejudicial to the realm, and even envisaged a time when it would 'not remayne destitute of an heire that may be a fitt governor'; but concluded with the prophecy that it would 'in the end' be sufficient that a marble stone should declare 'that a Queene, having raigned such a tyme, lived and dyed a virgin' (Hartley, 1.44–5). Despite those memorable words, the speech had more openness to the possibility of marriage than a different version provided by Camden, in which she is supposed to have chided the Commons for forgetting that she was already married to her kingdom, with a little dumbshow involving her coronation ring.

Elizabeth had no lack of suitors, including Philip II, Erik XIV of Sweden, and the archdukes Ferdinand and Charles of Austria. The more the merrier, since each proposal was an endorsement of her legitimacy. Erik was the most persistent suitor, and the most generous. A series of Swedish missions between summer 1559 and autumn 1562 came laden with 'massy bullion' and stables worth of piebald horses (Nichols, 1.79–82, 87, 104–5). Initial interest in Erik was a counterfoil to the more plausible candidature of the emperor Ferdinand's sons, Ferdinand and Charles. Charles, who symbolized an anti-French, Habsburg alliance, proved to have staying power, but religion was an almost insuperable bar, and it was one which was exploited for all that it was worth by the man whom Elizabeth would probably have chosen to marry if all things had been equal, Dudley. What kept Erik's hopes alive into 1562 was hostility to Dudley and his ambition; and it does seem that what kept all international suits at the level of diplomatic games was Elizabeth's genuine love for this man who was destined to be the longest running of her favourites, if never her spouse.

Elizabeth's relationship with Robert Dudley

Elizabeth's 'affair' with Dudley is the stuff of which legends are made, and have been, by Sir Walter Scott and many others. Dudley was a married man, otherwise things might have been both less and more complicated. The couple were of an age, and Dudley claimed to have known Elizabeth 'familierement' from before she was eight (Doran, *Monarchy and Matrimony*, 40). While Dudley's wife, Amy, *née* Robsart, was still alive, courtiers exchanged scandalous gossip about his relationship with the queen.

Even as rumours spread, on 8 September 1560 at Cumnor Place, Oxfordshire, Amy Dudley was found dead in unusual and even suspicious circumstances. Was it suicide or murder? Modern science has found a plausible, if not conclusive, medical explanation. With Amy dead, many assumed that Elizabeth would marry her favourite. How far Dudley's chances of marrying Elizabeth were realistic depends in part upon the reading of some very complicated diplomatic transactions, relating to whether England would opt to participate in the third assembly of the Council of Trent, whether Philip could be persuaded to favour Dudley's suit as the price for a return of England to the Catholic fold, whether proposals along these lines were made to the Spanish ambassador, Alvaro de la Quadra, bishop of Aquila, and, if so, whether they were made with sincerity. While there is no historical consensus on this matter, it appears most likely that Elizabeth's and Dudley's diplomatic games with the ambassador were just that, games. For Elizabeth was unlikely to tear up her religious settlement, while Dudley later claimed, with apparent sincerity, to have been consistent in his protestantism, 'ever from my cradle brought up in it' (Collinson, *Godly People*, 95). As for Cecil, it should not be assumed that he was motivated by simple hostility to Dudley.

It is more than likely that in the months after Amy Dudley's death, Elizabeth decided that marriage with Dudley was not on. This would mean that, unlike Mary, queen of Scots, in 1565, her head and political instincts came to rule her heart. However, Dudley continued to apply what might be termed cultural pressure. Sir Thomas Smith's 'Dialogue on the queen's marriage', which circulated in manuscript, John Philip's *The Play of Patient Grissell*, and, above all, *Gorboduc*, the Senecan tragedy written by Thomas Sackville and Thomas Norton and performed in the Inner Temple at Christmas 1561, and subsequently at court, all implicitly advocated the Dudley match.

When parliament next met in January 1563, it was in the shadow of Elizabeth's close encounter with death through smallpox in October 1562. Marriage and the succession were therefore at the top of the agenda for both houses, while the dean of St Paul's Cathedral, Alexander Nowell, one of the queen's favourite divines, preached a sermon to parliament which could hardly have been more direct. If her parents had been of her mind, not to marry, where would she have been then? The Lords petitioned her to marry 'where it shall please you, with whom it shall please yow, and assone as it shall please you' (Hartley, 1.59). The Commons placed more emphasis on the need to limit the succession. More answers answerless. Elizabeth told parliament that so far as her marriage was concerned 'a silent thoght may serve', but that the idea that she would never marry was a 'heresie' they should put out of their minds (ibid., 114). Yet, that she would never marry Dudley was probably not a heresy. When she made him Baron Denbigh on 28 September 1564 and earl of Leicester on the 29th, it was to make him acceptable as a husband for Mary, a plan which misfired when the Scottish queen married Lord Henry Darnley on 29 July 1565. Thereafter Leicester remained in the wings with little prospect of gaining the prize himself. The elaborate allegories enacted in Elizabeth's presence at Leicester's castle at Kenilworth in 1575 were aimed as much at securing his release from a kind of courtly bondage (so that he could himself marry and secure an heir) as to press an ever more unattainable suit.

The Habsburg matrimonial project was now revived. It is perhaps surprising that Cecil was so much and for so long in favour of this marriage, since it was clear that the archduke Charles was not likely to change his religion, and it could only have happened on the basis of an interpretation of the religion of England which would have been unacceptable to all but the most conservative of protestants. Despite this, Elizabeth clearly signalled to Vienna in May 1565 her intention to marry, with the implication that her choice would be the archduke. When parliament met again, in September 1566, key figures were poised to assure those now inclined to press for a resolution of the succession problem that she intended to marry. At this point Elizabeth came dangerously close to committing herself to marriage in order to stave off public debate about the succession; but she had an escape route, which was to dissolve (rather than prorogue) parliament, and when Cecil and others inserted a clause in a draft of the preamble to the subsidy bill referring to the promise to marry and acknowledging the legitimacy of public concern about the succession, her indignant reaction led to its prompt removal.

When Thomas Radcliffe, third earl of Sussex, was dispatched to Vienna to resume serious negotiations, his task was to persuade Maximilian II that the religion of England was not Calvinist but consistent with the Lutheranism of the Augsburg confession (since 1555 legal in the empire), so that there would be no need for Charles to insist on the practice of his own religion, something on which, however, Vienna did insist. In order to keep the negotiations alive, Sussex went beyond his remit on these critical matters. In England both a divided privy council and Elizabeth were forced to admit that even the limited, private practice of Catholicism would be unacceptable to the protestant public. Mary's deposition on 24 July 1567 was an event still fresh in everyone's memory. In December 1567 Elizabeth called the whole thing off. It proved too divisive and politically hazardous, and its subtext was open hostility between Sussex and Leicester, an overture to the major political crisis of 1569.

Last matrimonial proposals

The two French marriage projects of the 1570s, to Henri, duc d'Anjou, from 1570 to 1571 and to his brother François, duc d'Alençon (himself duc d'Anjou from 1578), between 1572 and 1582, were repeat performances, insofar as both matches appeared to be diplomatically advantageous, and both were torpedoed by the same religious factor. There were, however, other impediments, including traditional anti-French sentiment, and the disparity in age between Elizabeth and the French princes. Despite these difficulties, the queen may have been in earnest in her dealings with Henri of Anjou and his mother, Catherine de' Medici, and domestically the first Anjou marriage negotiation was not an especially divisive issue. However, the later episodes in François of Alençon and Anjou's long-running suit were another matter. England in the late 1570s confronted a number of dangers, variously assessed by those in charge of its affairs. In January 1576 it was said that 'hire Majestie is troubled with these causes, which maketh hire verie malincolie; and simeth greatlie to be oute of quiate' (Lodge, 2.136). France was either the old enemy or the only 'stay' against the new enemy, Spain, its support to be secured either by marriage or a 'league'. However, England was vulnerable because of the situation in Scotland and Ireland and Anjou was unreliable, especially because of his intervention in the Dutch revolt. The Elizabethan regime was divided about whether or not to intervene in the Low Countries. Elizabeth pulled back from the brink of military intervention, the preferred policy of the would-be warlord, Leicester, and of Sir Francis Walsingham, principal secretary. Marriage to Anjou, or talk of marriage, would at least buy time.

Yet there was more to this affair than diplomacy. To the surprise and alarm of many, when Anjou sent his servant Jean de Simier, baron de Saint-Marc, to act the ardent lover in his place, the 45-year-old Elizabeth seemed to be swept off her feet. Through much of 1579, court, privy council, and country were divided by the Anjou match. In May 1578 Gilbert Talbot, Lord Talbot, told his father, George Talbot, sixth earl of Shrewsbury, that odds of three to one were offered against the marriage. Now the odds shortened. Protestant opinion was outraged. For the hot protestant Nicholas Faunt, Walsingham's secretary and clerk of the signet, writing in March 1582, the marriage would be 'but treason' (Birch, 1.20). Leicester and his friends were opposed, and not only from self-interest, for the earl was one of those who expressed what sounds like genuine concern about the medical implications of Elizabeth marrying at her age, and suspected politically motivated manipulation of her emotions.

38 Baron Burghley (Cecil) wrote a hundred sheets of memoranda on the subject, for and against the marriage, which are preserved among the Hatfield manuscripts, and gave a speech on 6 October 1579 opposing it. However, the evidence is ambivalent and at times he seems to have supported Sussex, the principal proponent of the marriage. His judgement was perhaps swayed by the belief that England's diplomatic needs could not be secured without a marriage, the fact that this was the very last (risky) chance to secure an heir of the queen's body, and his conviction that the Anjou marriage would serve as a prophylactic against Mary, queen of Scots.

In the backlash of Elizabeth's indignant reaction to Leicester's marriage to Lettice Devereux, *née* Knollys, dowager countess of Essex, on 21 September 1578, Anjou visited the English court in person, the only one of the queen's foreign suitors to do so. He found Elizabeth either romantically interested or acting her part well. She called him her frog. Soon the proposed marriage was boldly denounced by the lawyer John Stubbe in *The Discoverie of a Gaping Gulf whereinto England is Like to be Swallowed* (1579). In what looked like a conspiracy, the book was widely disseminated. The queen suspected that greater persons than Stubbe were behind this, but historians have found in him a striking example of the existence of a public sphere in Elizabethan England, occupied and articulated by middle-ranking lawyers and politicians. Both Stubbe and the man who organized the distribution, William Page, a client of Francis Russell, second earl of Bedford, had their right hands struck off by the public hangman, which Camden recorded as a deeply unpopular sentence. Less publicly, the marriage was opposed by Sir Philip Sidney in an open letter and, obliquely, in Edmund Spenser's *The Shepheardes Calender* and in his more overt beast fable, *Mother Hubberd's Tale* (not published until 1591).

By October 1579 the conciliar argument against the marriage prevailed and Elizabeth knew that if she were to proceed it would be without the support of her privy council. In the last resort it was, after all, her decision, and for her privy councillors to say as much was not entirely a cop-out. This was effectively checkmate, although the project had an afterlife which finally petered out in the summer of 1581—as late as May 1582 Elizabeth still addressed Anjou as 'my dearest' (*Collected Works*, 237, 245, 249, 251, 253). A marriage treaty was concluded which everyone knew would never be implemented, not even when Anjou made a second and more public visit to England. As the biological clock ticked out of time, that was the end of matrimonial diplomacy. If time had been bought, reputations had been damaged, not least Elizabeth's own, and harm done, especially to Scottish policy. Walsingham wrote in 1578: 'no one thing hath procured her so much hatred as these wooing matters, as that it is conceived she dallieth therein' (Read, *Walsingham*, 2.6).

The struggle for stability

4

The Virgin Queen

It was in the context of the Anjou courtship, and as an expression of opposition to it, that the persona of the Virgin Queen was invented, or at least perfected. On the royal progress into East Anglia in 1578, plays and masques devised by Thomas Churchyard were performed at Norwich which celebrated Elizabeth's admirable virginity, with appropriate reference to Diana and the Virgin Mary. A year later Spenser deployed similar allegorical imagery in *The Shepheardes Calender*, and a series of portraits rubbed the same point home with the symbol of a sieve held in the queen's hand, which identified her with the vestal virgin Tuccia, who had employed a sieve full of water to prove her chastity.

As with her religion, Elizabeth's emotional and sexual history is hard to disentangle from diplomacy and artifice. Was she really a virgin? Many of her subjects doubted it. Nor was the gossip confined to the alehouse and the lower orders. In an utterly scandalous letter, perhaps written in 1584, Mary, queen of Scots, enjoying the enforced hospitality of the earl and countess of Shrewsbury at Sheffield, chose to make mischief by sharing with Elizabeth what she had heard from the countess, Elizabeth Talbot: how someone to whom Elizabeth had promised herself in matrimony often slept with her (possibly Leicester); that she would never marry Anjou, since she would never forgo her freedom to make love with her favourites, including Sir Christopher Hatton. Mary, of course, believed none of this but thought that Elizabeth ought to be told. It is perhaps more intriguing still that Elizabeth's godson, Sir John Harington, chose to present her with an epigram 'Of King David', which drew a moral from David's adultery with Bathsheba. This is not evidence that Elizabeth was a nymphomaniac but an indication of what some people were prepared to believe. However, was it significant that when she faced death in the autumn of 1562, she settled the unusually generous legacy of £500 on the groom of the privy chamber, John Tamworth, keeper of the privy purse, who perhaps knew more than others what might have been going on, and named Dudley as protector of the realm? The only evidence for this comes from the often unreliable de Quadra, who affirmed that 'nothing improper had ever passed between them' (Hume, 1.263).

Historians and biographers have praised Elizabeth for choosing celibacy but, leaving aside the question of how far that choice was simply hers, as long as she remained single and without heirs of her own body she gambled with the succession on the stake of her own life. As a speaker in the Commons put it in 1567: 'if God should take her Majestie, the succession being not established, I know not what shall become of my self, my wife, my children, landes, goodes, friendes or cuntrie' (Hartley, 1.138). In 1572, when the point at issue was the execution of Mary, queen of Scots, another MP demanded: 'since the Queene in respect of her owne safety is not to bee induced hereunto, let us make petition shee will doe it in respect of our safety' (ibid., 376). This was also an exclusion crisis, since to limit the succession was to exclude Mary. The pitting of the interests of subject and monarch against one another was debilitating from the royal perspective and enabling for the wider political nation.

The royal issue: public opinion and the Scottish queen

In the absence of an heir of her body, Elizabeth's successor ought to have been the next heir presumptive, but a confused legal situation meant that the identity of such an heir could not be presumed and was likely to be contested, unless the situation could be clarified by further legislation, a course of action against which the queen consistently set her face. Henry's third and final Succession Act of 1544 provided for an orderly succession through Edward, Mary, and Elizabeth. In case none of these should have lawful issue, Henry was empowered to further limit the succession by letters patent or his will.

Henry's last will, of 30 December 1546, made the next heir his niece Frances Grey, née Brandon (1517–1559), elder daughter of his younger sister, Mary (1496–1533), widow of Louis XII of France. Frances married Henry Grey, duke of Suffolk. If she had no children, her sister Eleanor (1519–1547), who was married to Henry Clifford, second earl of Cumberland, would be heir. In fact Frances had three daughters: Jane (1537–1554) [Lady Jane Dudley], who was proclaimed queen, deposed, and executed; Katherine (1540?–1568) [Katherine Seymour]; and Mary. Henry's will by its silence on the matter excluded the Stewart descendants of his elder sister, Margaret (1489–1541), dowager queen of Scotland, whose title passed down to Mary, queen of Scots (Margaret's granddaughter and Elizabeth's second cousin), and to the family of Margaret's second marriage, including Darnley, who had the advantage of English birth and whose marriage to Mary made of the senior and junior Stewart lines one flesh.

With Elizabeth's accession, and for as long as she remained childless, Katherine Grey had an apparent statutory right to succeed, since Henry's will was annexed to the Succession Act. Mary Stewart had the stronger hereditary claim. However, not only Henry's will but the common law with respect to aliens was prejudicial to her position in the order of succession, which was complicated further by Henri II's refusal to acknowledge Elizabeth's legitimacy, claiming for Mary the title and arms of England, by her marriage to François II from 1558 to 1560, and, most of all and increasingly in the perception of English protestants, by the fact that she was a Catholic.

The contest was originally between the hereditary claim of the Catholic and foreign Mary and the statutory claim of the protestant native, Katherine. Katherine's chances of being recognized by Elizabeth as her successor were probably never very good, and they were blown away when, in August 1561, it was found that she was pregnant, having secretly married Edward Seymour, first earl of Hertford. The couple were sent to the Tower on 5 September 1561. Mary returned to Scotland on 19 August 1561 and began to press her claim through Sir William Maitland of Lethington. Maitland failed to extract from Elizabeth recognition of the queen of Scots as her heir presumptive but she made no secret of her preference for Mary. As for the other claimants: 'Alas! What power or force have any of them, poor souls?' (Levine, 32). Elizabeth's refusal to name a successor, another of her *semper eadems*, was in her own interest, since as the 'second person' in her sister's reign she more than anyone had experience of the double threat which that posed. It was not seen to be in the interest of her people.

So some people resorted to propaganda and agitation, both direct and indirect. *Gorboduc* (January 1562) contrived to be about the not entirely compatible claims of Dudley to marry the queen and of Katherine Grey to succeed her. Parliament met a year later, and the Commons in its petition that Elizabeth both marry and limit the succession made no secret of its opposition to the Marian claim, if only on religious grounds, and asked the queen either to publish the terms of Henry's will if it provided the 'certainty' required, or to provide that certainty if it did not (Hartley, 1.90–93). The outlook was in fact so uncertain, and the queen so seriously ill with smallpox, that Cecil devised an extraordinary, stopgap solution to the problem, in the form of arrangements for a legalized interregnum. This constitutionally radical scheme effectively distinguished between the queen's natural body and her body politic, which could, if only temporarily, be detached from the physical life and person of the monarch and vested in a public, conciliar body. Elizabeth's own solution, a plan which was radical in a different and thoroughly inscrutable way, and dead in the water almost from the outset, was to arrange a marriage between Dudley and Mary which might sugar the pill of the Scottish succession.

Now a long-running pamphlet war began, Katherine's claims versus Mary's claims, in which John Hales, MP for Lancaster in 1563, fired the first shot, in a tract intended perhaps in its original form to sway parliament. Robert Beale and Sir Nicholas Bacon, lord keeper of the great seal and Cecil's brother-in-law, were involved. Elizabeth suspected a widespread conspiracy and steps were taken to indict Hales for presumptuously initiating a debate on 'the right, title, limitation, and succession of the

Imperial Crown of England' (Levine, 72). Responses from the other side included a treatise by the eminent Catholic jurist Edmund Plowden and the *Defence* of Mary (1569) by John Leslie, bishop of Ross. These arguments hinged on whether the succession could be settled by inheritance or by statute but more potent, politically, was the growing prejudice against Mary, and not just because of her religion. Katherine's party was winning the war of words but her death on 27 January 1568 and the lack of a suitably convincing alternative snatched defeat from the jaws of victory.

Meanwhile dramatic events in Scotland blasted Mary's reputation in the eyes of the world: the murder of Darnley, her marriage to one of his murderers in a Calvinist wedding ceremony, rebellion, defeat, and enforced abdication in favour of the infant James VI (1566–1625). Elizabeth offered Mary frank advice, following 'the abominable murder of your mad husband and my killed cousin'. Four months later she wrote:

> How could a worse choice be made for your honour than in such haste to marry such a subject [James Hepburn, fourth earl of Bothwell], who . . . public fame hath charged with the murder of your late husband? . . . This you see plainly, what we think of the marriage.

Three years later she wrote: 'Well I will overpass your hard accidents that followed for lack of following of my counsels' (*Collected Works*, 116, 118, 123).

Only when Mary escaped from captivity to take refuge in England on 16 May 1568 did she manage to persuade many Catholics of her innocence and orthodoxy. By the end of 1568, again a captive, Mary represented the alternative to the protestant ascendancy in England. Consequently, the political forces of that ascendancy were now to be concentrated on her exclusion from the succession by fair means or foul. However, protestants had no plausible candidate of their own and were stuck with a mere negation. The problem of the succession was placed on uneasy hold, for at no time, before or after Mary's execution on 8 February 1587, would Elizabeth allow it to be publicly discussed, whether in parliament or anywhere else.

Success in Scotland, failure in France

While much of the politics of the first decade of Elizabeth's reign concerned the question of what might succeed it, historians who know that her reign had forty-five years to run have enjoyed a different perspective. Aware of what the future held, they have made a teleology of the early years of uncertainty, foreign adventures, and still fragile and untested political alliances, aware that what was coming next was a major crisis at the end of the decade, the acid test of the Elizabethan regime, to be followed by relative stability in the 1570s. All these events were a mere overture to a partly invented Elizabethan golden age.

Elizabeth was credited by her earliest historians, and even on her funerary monument in Westminster Abbey, with a limited number of outstanding and historic achievements. Foremost among these was the religious settlement, and after that the reform of the currency, much abused by Henry's and Edward's financial policies, which she set in motion as early as February 1559, a process involving calling in debased coins in exchange for new, finer ones and a devaluation. It was easy on a tombstone to represent these as tidy and decisive reforms. Tidy they were not. The religious settlement could be said to have settled nothing, and to have left loose ends which remained entangled for the next two hundred years. The recoinage and devaluation took nearly two years to achieve, disturbed the markets, alarmed consumers, and failed to deal with inflationary pressures on the economy. Yet these reforms were certainly decisive, a decisiveness not always associated with Elizabeth. The question, as always, is, was the decisiveness hers or that of others?

Even more decisive and momentous was Elizabeth's intervention in Scotland in 1559–60, and here it was certainly Cecil rather than his mistress who favoured bold and swift action. The opportunity was created by the violent turn taken by the Scottish Reformation, a revolution headed by disaffected magnates who called themselves the lords of the congregation and intended to overthrow both the old religion and French domination, under the regent Mary of Guise. But it was a revolution which could succeed only with English military and financial aid, which was duly requested. This was an opportunity, wrote Cecil, which, if missed, would not come again in his lifetime. As a veteran of Somerset's aggressive Scottish policy, Cecil had the vision of a British state, Scotland either 'in a perpetuall peace with the kingdom of Ingland or to be made one Monarchie with England as they both make but one Ile devided from the rest of the world' (Alford, 223). It was all too probable that the alternative to action would not be the *status quo* but French mastery of England itself, the ambition of the dominant French faction, the Guise family. English intervention in the maelstrom of Scottish politics and in support of a rebellion against a sovereign government which seemed likely to fail was a high risk and expensive policy towards which Cecil, by all the rhetorical forces at his command, had to convince first himself, then his fellow privy councillors, and finally a reluctant queen, whom he cajoled every foot of the way and blackmailed with threats of resignation. He wrote, in May 1560, when the English forces sent to assist the insurgency had suffered a severe setback in their assault on the French garrison in Leith: 'the Queen's Majesty never liketh this matter of Scotland' (MacCaffrey, *Shaping*, 83).

In consequence, Cecil took the greatest risk of his career when he travelled to Edinburgh with Dr Nicholas Wotton to negotiate with the Scots and the French in June 1560. A happy conjunction of accidents, including the death of Mary of Guise on 11 June, enabled him to conclude the treaty of Edinburgh on 6 July, which effectively ended the 'auld alliance' with France and looked forward to a permanent pacification, if not a political union, of the island of Britain: a truly historic moment. It was followed by the formal adoption of protestantism by the Scottish parliament.

What Elizabeth's tombstone did not record among her achievements was that she restored Calais to her dominions. This was not achieved by the somewhat humiliating peace concluded with France at Cateau Cambrésis on 3 April 1559, but it was something which she deeply desired, and for the sake of which she was prepared to place at risk the settlement of Scotland. It was in part to keep the question of Calais on the agenda that in 1562 Elizabeth, although as ever 'loath to adventure' (MacCaffrey, 'The Newhaven expedition', 9–10), sanctioned intervention in the first of the French wars of religion by sending an expeditionary force to Newhaven (Le Havre) to hold it for the Huguenots. Newhaven was to be a pledge for the return of Calais. However, a more overt reason for the intervention was to bolster the cause of French protestantism and to offset Spanish support for the contrary faction, headed by the Guise family, the French relations of Mary, queen of Scots. It no doubt helped to dispel Elizabeth's doubts that the Newhaven expedition was enthusiastically backed by Dudley, whom she appointed to her privy council in October 1562, and commanded by his brother, Ambrose Dudley, earl of Warwick; whereas it was now Cecil's turn to be all too aware of the dangers involved.

In the event, this piece of decisiveness was as unsuccessful as Cecil's Scottish war and peace had been successful. Unable to play a meaningful military role and sinking ever deeper into a diplomatic morass, the English were soon regarded as unwelcome intruders by both French sides. Finally, bubonic plague more than decimated the expeditionary force, which took the infection back to England as it withdrew. Although this had been a costly humiliation, it did not drive Elizabeth's realm into isolationism. England's participation in Europe's religious wars, and especially the unofficial part played by 'volunteers', was only just beginning. The confused diplomatic incident of 1568, which involved the English seizure of the treasure ships destined to deliver the silver bullion Fernando Álvarez de Toledo, third duke of Alba, needed to wage war in the Netherlands, was a pointer to the future, a future in which Spain rather than France would be perceived to be the enemy.

Conspiracy and rebellion

For the remainder of the decade the Elizabethan regime remained fragile, vulnerable, and lacking in direction, reactive rather than proactive. The leading political players, including Cecil, Sussex, Thomas Howard, fourth duke of Norfolk, Leicester, and his friends, were all uncertain where they stood relationally, a case of frictions if not quite of organized factions. There was no solution to the conundrum of the succession. Elizabeth herself was still learning how to be queen.

In 1568 she was faced with the toughest decision of her reign, and one with which she had to live for the next eighteen years: what to do with Mary, who in that year landed on her doorstep. To restore Mary to her Scottish kingdom (Elizabeth's own preferred policy), to allow her to return to France, where she was dowager queen, or to keep her in detention in England, all were potentially dangerous options. A commission of inquiry into the issues between Mary and her half-brother, James Stewart, earl of Moray, now regent in Scotland, became, in effect, her first English trial, although it was Moray who was formally in the dock. Moray's exploitation of the casket letters between Mary and Bothwell may seem lurid but the inquiry was inconclusive and Elizabeth had no choice but to continue to accommodate her cousin as the most uncomfortable of house guests. For Catholics she was a symbol of hope. Protestants, who had no doubt as to her sexual, religious, and political guilt, soon began to demand her head on a charger.

Paradoxically, it would take a political earthquake—the events of 1569 to 1572—to invest Elizabeth's government with greater stability and confidence. It began with the idea of a marriage between Mary and England's premier nobleman, Norfolk. Mary, with Norfolk, would return to Scotland and in due course succeed Elizabeth in England. France and Spain would be neutralized. This was a plan which had much going for it, and it was supported from across the political spectrum by, among others, Leicester (albeit, in Camden's prejudiced opinion, from devious motives), but not by Cecil, who was intended to be its first victim. It was a web which began to unravel as soon as it was spun, particularly at the Scottish end, and no one dared to tell Elizabeth. When she was informed, all too late in the day, Norfolk was on the carpet. He lost his nerve and withdrew to his East Anglian estates, disobeying repeated summonses to return to court. When he did return it was to temporary custody in the Tower, while his fellow conspirators made their peace with the queen as best they could. Suddenly there could be no doubt who was in charge of Elizabethan England.

Among Norfolk's disappointed abetters were the northern earls, Thomas Percy, sixth earl of Northumberland, and Charles Neville, sixth earl of Westmorland, and in the aftermath of the Norfolk match, conspiracy lurched over the edge into outright rebellion, a rising with echoes of the Pilgrimage of Grace of 1536 and the last of its kind. Much of the far north was in the hands of the rebels from November 1569 and the symbols of protestantism were purged from Durham Cathedral on 14 November. Faced with the will of the Tudor state, an iron will in such a crisis as this, and with Mary removed beyond reach, the northern uprising was scotched, literally, as its leaders crossed into Scotland. Of the rank-and-file followers, forced to stay behind, hundreds were hanged in their own villages. There was an aftershock in the secondary rising of Leonard Dacre, which it needed a small battle to suppress, won on 20 February 1570 by Elizabeth's cousin Hunsdon, who was congratulated as 'the instrument of my glory' (*Collected Works*, 126).

Finally, in this watershed for the regime, the international dimension came into play: first a pro-Marian reaction in Scotland, following Moray's assassination on 21 January 1570 (a reaction soon reversed); and more or less simultaneously, in the early months of 1570, *Regnans in excelsis*, Pius V's bull, which impotently presumed to deprive Elizabeth of her throne and to release her subjects from their bonds of allegiance. Despite this, negotiations for Mary's restoration to her Scottish throne were going well when the first international plot against Elizabeth was uncovered, the extensive but flimsy web of conspiracy woven by the Italian Roberto di Ridolfi in 1570 and 1571, a hairbrained thing that implicated, if not Mary, her agents, the pope, the Spanish ambassador, Guerau de Spes, Alba's Spanish forces in the Netherlands, and Norfolk, who had not yet learned his lesson.

Cecil's exposure of all the ramifications of the Ridolfi plot confirmed the worst suspicions of protestant supporters of the regime while it had a transforming effect on Elizabeth's attitude towards her cousin, anatomized in verses which the queen wrote about this time as:

The daughter of debate
That discord aye doth sow.
(*Collected Works*, 134)

Cecil instructed Mary's keeper, Shrewsbury, to 'tempt' her with assurances that Elizabeth could well understand why she had taken steps to secure her own liberty and to marry her son to the Spanish infanta and herself to Don John of Austria. However, Shrewsbury was also instructed to conceal Elizabeth's indignation at Mary's 'labors and devises to stirre up a new rebellion in this realme, and to have the Kynge of Spayne to asist it'. In this way Mary would be lured into confessing things which Elizabeth already knew 'by wrytyng extant' (Lambeth Palace London, MS 3197, fol. 33).

When parliament met in May 1572, Elizabeth allowed publication of a version of the incriminating casket letters and Norfolk was found guilty of treason, although the queen, with qualms which would never have afflicted her father, hesitated to send him to the scaffold. Parliament demanded the heads of both Mary and Norfolk. The bishops were instructed virtually to threaten Elizabeth with divine deposition if she failed to execute Mary, just as God punished Saul for his failure to kill the pagan Agag, with loss of his throne to David and his descendants. The most probable author of this ultimatum, Edwin Sandys, bishop of London, put first among measures for the public safety 'furthwith to cutte of the Scottish Quene's heade: *ipsa est nostri fundi calamitas*' ('she is the calamity of our land'; Ellis, 2nd ser., 3.25). Norfolk went to the block on 2 June 1572 but the queen resisted extreme pressure to execute Mary, preferring an act rather than an axe: that is, an act disabling the former queen of Scots from succeeding to the English throne. The Commons did not like this because a disabling act would tacitly recognize that Mary had a claim. In the end, Elizabeth put it off. As the dust settled, the leading figures in government established more stable relationships and Cecil and Leicester were not always factional rivals. With Walsingham, they formed an unusually coherent conciliar regime, which was more often divided from Elizabeth than within itself.

5 Court and country

Courtiers and councillors

The Elizabeth who has become almost a historical cliché has been romanticized as a kind of queen bee at the centre of a hive populated by glittering and competing favourites. Distinctions have been drawn between on the one hand 'mere' favourites, decorative players like, above all, Leicester, Sir Christopher Hatton, who was thought to have made it to the high office of lord chancellor by his performance on the dance floor, and Sir Walter Ralegh, and, on the other, workaholic politicians, more soberly dressed, such as Burghley and Walsingham. This crude dichotomy is unhelpful. All privy councillors were, in some measure, courtiers, and if all courtiers were not privy councillors that makes the point that it was at court that politics was conducted. Leicester, the arch-courtier, was not a member of the privy council when he persuaded Elizabeth of the merits of the Newhaven expedition. It was said, by Burghley, that when the queen turned against Edmund Grindal, she listened more to her Italian doctor, Giulio Borgarucci, an interested party, than to any member of the privy council. The cliché ignores Hatton's long political apprenticeship and underestimates his considerable ability; while Leicester, thanks to his many enemies, has been unfairly dismissed and vilified, the power which he exercised, especially the power of patronage, not acknowledged for what it was, an important structural component of the regime.

This configuration of the Elizabethan court was in part the invention of Sir Robert Naunton who, writing about 1630, organized his *Fragmenta regalia, or, Observations on the Late Queen Elizabeth* as an account of favourites. Historians have been too ready to accept Naunton's claim that 'the principall note' of the reign was that the queen 'ruled much by faction and parties, which her self both made, upheld, and weakened, as her own great judgement advised' (*Sir Robert Naunton*, 16, 18). For Naunton's little book was a disguised commentary on the unsatisfactory politics of the 1620s. It is not the case that the Elizabethan court, throughout a long reign, was always clearly divided into factions and parties, still less that this divisiveness was a deliberate contrivance of Elizabeth's 'great judgement'. There is evidence that she knew how to preserve her freedom of manoeuvre by playing off one interest against another, but just as often she confronted a privy council which as a body was of a mind different from her own. Nor was Elizabeth enthroned above the frictions and factions of her court. Her variable likes, dislikes, and emotions were often more part of the destabilizing problem than of the solution.

This is not to deny that the centre of Elizabethan political activity consisted of personalities and personal relations. Elizabeth found nicknames for her leading courtiers: 'Eyes' for Leicester, for example, written as two little circles with eyebrows, 'Lids' for Hatton; and her relations with these favourites were conducted according to the codes of courtly love and mock worship. Friendship and favour (not to speak of their opposite, enmity) were the values around which court life revolved, marked and symbolized in such rituals as the exchange of new year gifts, the balance of payments somewhat unequal, the gifts carefully adjusted to the rank, standing, and wealth of donors and recipients. Over her first eleven years, the queen received gifts valued at £11,905 5*s*. 2*d*., her own gifts at £8400 11*s*. 1½*d*. From the late 1570s, as 17 November began to be almost a religious feast, there were accession day tilts at court, in which nobles and knights jousted in competition for Elizabeth's favour. Christmas was a season of misrule, which had its paradoxical function in affirming the proper order of things. In 1562 nine or ten couples of hounds were let loose to hunt a fox and a cat around the hall, with both animals 'killed beneath the fire' (Nichols, 1.139). In 1600 it was reported that over the Christmas holidays the queen had almost every night come into the presence chamber 'to see the Ladies dawnce the old and new cowntry Dawnces, with the Taber and Pipe' (Arnold, 97). There was also 'primero' and other card games, played for high stakes. The accounts for 1576 of Roger North, second Baron North, record amounts as high as £70, 'lost at play with the queen' (Nichols, 2.241).

Almost all Elizabeth's leading men were at times the victims of her extreme anger. When Leicester exceeded the terms of his commission by accepting the governor-generalship of the Netherlands in February 1586, she wrote that she could never have imagined that a man whom she had created from nothing could have so contemptibly disobeyed her commandment. However, it was Elizabeth who took steps to heal this breach, and within six months she was writing: 'Rob, I am afraid you will suppose by my wandering writings that a midsummer moon hath taken large possession of my brains this month' (*Collected Works*, 282).

Often Elizabeth's relations with her men were whimsical and playful. On one occasion she prescribed a spartan diet for Leicester, including on festival days 'the shoulder of a wren' for dinner, and for supper 'a leg of the same', but that in the case of his brother Warwick (who was fatter) the wren's leg could be 'abated' (*Collected Works*, 230–31). When the queen was embarrassed to be spotted at her window in her night attire, she later gave 'a great phyllyp [fillip] on the forehed' to the voyeur, Lord Talbot (Lodge, 2.170). The letters of condolence which had to be written so frequently to bereaved spouses and parents contain sincere sentiment. She was not above exploiting her femininity. When the Scottish ambassador, Sir James Melville, surprised her playing the virginals, she stopped, pretended to slap him, and said that 'she was not used to play before men, but when she was solitary, to shun melancholy' (Nichols, 1.293). Although depression was a chronic and recurrent condition, generally Elizabeth was affable, but she could also be irascible, and, above all, unpredictable. When on 1 February 1587 William Davison, principal secretary, came to her with papers to sign which included the warrant for Mary's execution, she congratulated him on having taken a walk in the park and said that he ought to do it more often. Yet within days she wanted him hanged.

Inner circles

What was the court for? It was above all a place for courtly rituals, such as the formal daily procession to the Chapel Royal; and for the physical display of majesty, the place where Elizabeth could be seen by foreign ambassadors as well as subjects, wearing the dazzling contents of her huge wardrobe, those excessively bejewelled costumes for which she served as a kind of clothes horse in the famous full-length portraits. Even though she was a late riser, not a morning person she said, it took two hours to put her together each day, and as long again to put her to bed. However, it may have been only on state occasions that the queen was displayed in the full finery of her robes of estate.

The court was, in Sir Geoffrey Elton's phrase, 'a point of contact' (Elton, 3.38–57). In a system of personal monarchy there was no substitute for access to the very person of the monarch, immediate or through a privileged intermediary. In a celebrated essay, 'The Elizabethan political scene' (1948), Sir John Neale peered beneath the Renaissance splendour to uncover the squalid, materialistic competition for place and profit which he believed to be the court's true *raison d'être*. There were simply not enough goodies to go round. Like war, life at court was mostly about boredom, as suitors waited and waited. As Spenser wrote:

> Full little knowest thou that hast not tried
> What Hell it is in suing long to bide.
> (E. Spenser, *Mother Hubberd's Tale*, ll. 895–6)

It was also about service, even servitude, before any significant office or other substantial reward was obtained; and it was about the crucial machinery of patronage and the greasing of palms. As competition grew ever fiercer, the general direction of public morality was downward and degenerative. In a refinement of Neale's argument, Wallace MacCaffrey agreed that the Elizabethan monarchy rested 'on the substantial pillars of its capacity to reward and advance its supporters', but he believed the system to have been benignly functional in cementing loyalty to the regime (Bindoff and others, 97). However, both essays had too little to say about how politics in something more like the modern sense was also transacted, and contested, at court.

Excessive attention bestowed on the greatest of the queen's men, her favourites, has distracted consideration from the many lesser men who constituted the personnel of her court, and from her women, as well as taking the place of any serious analysis of how the institution worked. At the heart of the court lay the privy lodgings, the living quarters of the monarch. Under Henry VIII, the gentlemen of the privy chamber were the companions of the king, and constituted a focal point of power, but under Mary and Elizabeth they were necessarily replaced by women. There were three or four ladies of the bedchamber, and a dozen or so ladies, gentlewomen, and maids of the privy chamber, with six maids of honour, teenagers under the supervision of the 'mother of the maids'. The most senior and long-lasting of these courtly women were Elizabeth's oldest and most constant friends: Blanche Parry, who had seen Elizabeth in her cradle and who died, still in her service, in 1590, Astley, Elizabeth Fiennes de Clinton, countess of Lincoln, Frances Seymour, countess of Hertford, Anne Dudley, countess of Warwick, and Mary Scudamore. The countess of Warwick told Walsingham in 1585 that she had 'spentt the cheffe partt of her yeares both painfully, faythfully, and servyceably' in the queen's household, and there were still many years to run (National Archives, SP 12/181/77).

These women were in constant attendance on Elizabeth, dressing her and attending to her most intimate needs, eating with her in the privy chamber, sewing. This enabled them to act on behalf of suitors, and no doubt at some personal profit. Beale, the clerk of the privy council, advised that when bringing business before the queen a principal secretary should learn 'her Majesties disposicion by some in the Privie Chamber, with whom you must keepe creditt, for that will stande you in much steede', while warning him not to yield too much to their 'importuntie for sutes' (Read, *Walsingham*, 1.437). Formally, these women had no political role, but no more than Naunton is Rowland Vaughan, Parry's great-nephew, to be believed when he wrote (again, motivated by Jacobean politics) that these great ladies concerned themselves only with 'little lay matters', 'to serve their freinds turnes', and 'durst [not] intermeddle so far in matters of commonwealth' (Vaughan, sigs. H*v*–H2*r*). It is almost inconceivable that they would not have 'intermeddled', especially in the politics of the queen's marital affairs, of which there is some hard evidence, especially from 1579. As for the maids, who slept together in a kind of dormitory, the court was a marriage market and a sexual minefield, judging by the numbers who faced disgrace and Elizabeth's anger when they were found to be pregnant or secretly married. There were many scandals between the affair of Katherine Grey in 1561 and Mary Fitton's case in the late 1590s. These liaisons and marriages were liable to involve Elizabeth's gentlemen pensioners, who were in constant attendance in the presence chamber. They were of greater social status than their predecessors under Henry and Edward because the office of gentleman of the privy chamber was no longer open to them. Many were related to the gentlewomen of the privy chamber. Appointment as a gentleman pensioner could lead to greater things. Hatton is a case in point. However, most senior courtiers remained in post throughout their careers. The countess of Lincoln was in Elizabeth's household from before 1538 until her death in 1590. One of the most remarkable features of the Elizabethan world is that almost nobody was sacked, or resigned, Davison being the most notable exception. There are verses set to music by John Dowland in 1603 which catch the spirit of the times:

Time stands still with gazing on her face.
Stand still and gaze, for minutes, hours and years to her give place.
All other things shall change but she remains the same,
Till heavens changed have their course and Time hath lost his name.
(E. H. Fellowes, ed., *English Madrigal Verse, 1585–1632*, rev. F. W. Sternfeld and D. Greer, 1967, 479)

The outward show

What of 'the people'? Posterity embellished a legend of spontaneous outpourings of love and devotion from the subjects of this paragon of a queen: the people 'running, flying, flocking to be blessed with the sight of her Gracious Countenance as oft as ever she came forth in Publicke', a monarch 'thinking it her greatest strength to be fortified with their love, and her greatest happinesse to make them happy', 'borne to possesse the hearts of her Subject'. These are the words not of the less fulsome Camden but of his translator Robert Norton, who thought it necessary to gild the former's lily, boosting Elizabeth's 'glorious Fame' (*Historie*, trans. Norton, sigs. A1*r*–A4*r*).

Elizabeth in procession may well have been a familiar sight in and around London, as she moved from one palace to another, by road or river, and displayed herself ceremonially when she returned to Whitehall to keep Christmas. There were set-piece encounters with poor subjects, especially on Maundy Thursday, when she washed the feet of as many poor women as the years of her age, and distributed clothing, loaves and fishes, claret, and purses containing the same number of silver pennies. The queen also had what might be called private friends among those who were not glittering courtiers: for example, John Lacy, a rich member of the Clothworkers' Company, who lived on the river at Putney, with whom she stayed for two or three nights at a time on at least thirteen occasions between 1578 and 1603.

The only opportunity to see Elizabeth for those living deeper into the provinces was the annual summer progress, which usually lasted ten weeks, and which never took the court further west than Bristol and Worcester or farther north than Coventry and Stafford. Even then, the greatest crowds greeting the queen were, inevitably, London crowds: estimated at 10,000 when she returned from Suffolk in 1561. Progresses were a logistical nightmare for those who had to organize them, especially since the decision where to go could be taken at almost the last moment. In July 1576 Lord Talbot reported that there was 'no certayntie' about the queen's summer itinerary, 'for these II or III dayes it hathe changed every V owers' (Lodge, 2.150). The progress was also an expensive embarrassment for the householders obliged to entertain Elizabeth and to think of a suitable present. The 1578 progress cost North £762. Yet for the ambitious, this was also an opportunity, so that some of the great prodigy houses of the age were built for the express purpose of receiving the queen. The climax of what might be called the princely kind of progress came in 1575, with the lavish entertainment laid on at Leicester's castle at Kenilworth, and celebrated in literary effusions by Robert Laneham and George Gascoigne.

In so far as progresses afforded the opportunity to meet people below the rank of gentleman, these were townspeople. The ritual routine was always the same: a rich gift presented by the mayor, a speech from the recorder, something laid on by the schoolboys. When, in 1565, the mayor of Coventry presented

Elizabeth with a purse containing £100 in gold, he assured her that it contained more besides: 'the hearts of all your loving subjects'. At Warwick in 1572 she told the recorder: 'Come hither, little Recorder. It was told me that youe wold be afraid to look upon me, or to speak boldly; but youe were not so fraid of me as I was of youe' (Nichols, 1.192, 315).

Matters of church and state

6

Protestant nonconformity

In a speech to parliament in 1589, Sir Christopher Hatton, the lord chancellor, said that at the beginning of her reign Elizabeth had 'placed hir Reformation as uppon a square stone to remayne constant' (Folger Shakespeare Library, MS V.b.303, pp. 183–6). The stone may have been square but it was very shaky. Even before the religious settlement of 1559 was made, the 'Device for alteration of religion' accurately forecast that it would be rejected on the one hand by 'the papist sect', and on the other by those who, dissatisfied with its moderation, would 'call the alteration *a cloaked papistry* or *a mingle-mangle*' (Gee, 196–7). Sir Nicholas Bacon opened the 1559 parliament with an inclusivist plea to eschew such divisive terms as heretic, schismatic, and papist and closed it with an even-handed warning addressed to 'those that be to swifte as those that be to slowe, those, I say, that goe before the lawe or beyond the lawe, as those that will not followe' (Hartley, 1.51). That was to draw a line in the sand which has been called the Elizabethan compromise. However, the religion of Elizabethan England and of its queen was protestant, not semi-protestant or semi-Catholic.

Nevertheless, the dynamic, interactive relation indicated by Bacon between those for whom the Elizabethan settlement was too much and those for whom it was too little worked itself out inexorably in the years to come. The stigma of 'puritan', which soon attached to the latter, was in origin, about 1565, a clever invention of exiled Catholic pamphleteers, intended as an insult to all protestants, 'hot puritans of the new clergy' (Trinterud, 6–7). It was soon adopted by conformist defenders of the settlement who deployed it, among other defamatory terms, against nonconformists, who rejected such prayer book ceremonies as vestments and the sign of the cross in baptism, refused as a matter of conscience to subscribe to the legitimacy of such things, and agitated, in parliament, in the press, and by other means, for 'further reformation'. The hot protestants for their part complained of 'papists', a category which embraced not only recusants but so-called 'church papists', closet Catholics whose outward conformity made them all the more suspect, and dangerous. So 'puritan' and 'papist' were not terms of taxonomic definition but abusive and fluid labels which progressively defined each other and fed upon each other, as well as serving both to erode and to construct the middle ground between these two extremes. Such was the basic landscape, the tectonic plates, of Elizabethan religion.

In principle, Elizabeth was even-handedly opposed to both these polarized constructions. Hatton told the 1589 parliament that it was duty bound to 'bridle' all, 'whether papists or puritanes', who were 'discontented' with the established religion (Hartley, 2.419–20). Aylmer informed his patron, Hatton, that his marching orders on elevation to the bishopric of London in 1576 had been 'to cut off…and to correct offenders on both sides which swerve from the right path of obedience' (H. Nicolas, 56). What did this mean in practice? It was Francis

Bacon, not Elizabeth herself, who said that her intention was not to make windows in men's souls, but no doubt he interpreted correctly the essence of her religious policy. Outward conformity would suffice and perhaps the queen's pragmatic tolerance went beyond that. It was no secret that several members of her yeomen of the guard, including their captain, Robert Seale, charged as they were on a daily basis with Elizabeth's physical protection, were secret adherents of the Family of Love. The drawing of curtains over the soul's windows was an article of faith for Familists, so what certainty can there be that Elizabeth was not herself a secret Familist, or at least a sympathizer?

Recusancy

Elizabeth's relatively conservative sympathies in matters of religion have already been noticed. Provided Catholics kept their heads down and offered no threat to her regality, they were relatively safe. Despite her experiences in her sister's reign, Elizabeth would never have used the words uttered in a petition of the Commons in 1563, when there were still plenty of Catholic MPs: 'we feare a faccion of heretickes in your realme, contentious and malicious papistes ... Their unkindness and cruelty we have tasted' (Hartley, 1.91–2). In the 1560s there was a considerable measure of effective toleration. In common with many of her subjects, Elizabeth counted known Catholics among her relations and constant companions, not least in the court itself, especially her favourite musicians, such as William Byrd. That lifelong trimmer Lord Henry Howard 'would come and continue at prayers when the Queene came, but otherwise would not endure them, seeming to performe the duty of a subject in attending on his prince at the one tyme, and at the other using his conscience' (*Diary of John Manningham*, 246).

The papal bull *Regnans in excelsis*, in excommunicating and deposing Elizabeth, inevitably transformed the situation, as did the mounting of a Catholic mission in its wake dedicated to the reconversion of England. The trials and executions of seminary priests, from the mid-1570s on, fostering a cult of martyrdom, and out and out recusancy on the part of a minority of Catholics, worked as mutually exacerbatory forces. Although political Catholicism had no more determined an opponent (for it threatened her throne and perhaps her life), Elizabeth was far from heading a protestant crusade against it. When her second parliament made it treason for office-holders to refuse the oath of supremacy on a second occasion, Elizabeth made sure that it would not be tendered twice. In 1571 parliament approved a bill (which seems to have originated with the bishops) 'concerning coming to the church and receiving of the Communion', which sharply increased the penalties for non-attendance, and for the first time proposed to enforce by statute annual reception of the sacrament (Neale, *Elizabeth I and her Parliaments, 1559–1581*, 192). This was to aim at the heart of non-recusant Catholicism, the strategy of 'church papists'. However, the queen vetoed the bill.

In 1581 parliament responded to an intensification of the perceived Catholic threat (this was in the aftermath of the mission of the Jesuits, Edmund Campion and Robert Persons) by preparing legislation which can only be called draconically anti-Catholic, a true penal code. It is a reasonable presumption that Elizabeth worked behind the scenes to mitigate the severity of what was proposed by both houses. In the terms of the bill 'to retain the Queen's majesty's subjects in their due obedience', as originally drafted, to celebrate mass would have been made a felony, carrying in principle the death penalty; to hear mass to incur penalties which would have extended to life imprisonment and the forfeiture of lands and goods. It must have been the queen who reduced the penalties for these offences to substantial fines. For all Catholics (but landowning Catholic families were meant) the penalty for refusal to go to church, the crime of recusancy, was sharply increased to £20 a month, and this was enacted. Moreover, parliament intended to make it treasonable to convert, or be converted, to Catholicism. At this point, Elizabeth appears to have been responsible for the crucial insertion in the bill of three words, 'for that intent'. Only if conversions occurred with the specific intent of withdrawing her subjects from their natural allegiance were they treasonable (Neale, *Elizabeth I and her Parliaments, 1559–1581*, 386–9). This legislation has been praised for distinguishing between being a Catholic and becoming a Catholic, and for formally reserving the death penalty for a civil rather than a religious offence. For this Elizabeth must evidently be given personal credit.

Holding the religious line

Elizabeth's religious antipathies were more naturally and instinctively expressed against 'hot Protestants'. Not only did she have a personal distaste for a religious style so different from her own, but she detected and feared in puritanism a dangerous sectarianism and a threat to her own authority more subtle than that offered by 'papists', even though puritans were always ready, on their own terms, to subscribe to the royal supremacy.

Elizabeth's religious sensibilities and prejudices were never better exposed than in a series of exchanges with bishops and other senior clergy when they appeared before her in the privy chamber at Somerset House in February 1585 to offer their clerical subsidy. Having referred to the campaign against the bishops in the Commons, currently sitting, she promised to defend them against these attacks, and that if it were shown that they were countenanced by some in the privy council she would 'uncouncil' some of them (who were probably present to hear her say so). She then complained that the bishops were allowing ministers to preach what they liked, 'some one way, some another'. It would be better if they would read the official homilies, 'for there is more learning in one of those than in twenty of some of their sermons'. She knew of evidence that Catholics were encouraged by the loose talk of some protestants, 'for I have heard that some of them of late have said that I was of no religion, neither hot [nor] cold, but such as one day would give God the vomit'. Against her Catholic enemies she could defend herself, 'but from a pretensed friend, good Lord deliver me'. When John Whitgift, archbishop of Canterbury, responded to the complaint of the hour, that there were not enough learned preachers and too many sub-standard clergy, protesting that to have a learned minister in every parish was impossible, since there were thirteen thousand parishes, the queen exploded: 'Jesus! ... thirteen thousand! It is not to be looked for'—nor, apparently, desired (*Collected Works*, 177–81).

Such things would probably not have been said in a more public forum. Elizabeth was well aware that she could not afford to flaunt godly opinion. In 1582 Thomas Bentley, a member of the very well-connected Gray's Inn circle, published *The Monument of Matrones*, 1600 closely printed pages on the religion of women. This was a celebration of the queen's exemplary piety, but it was also an almost threateningly prescriptive text, in which God was made to say to Elizabeth: 'beware therefore that yee abuse not this authoritie given unto you by me, under certaine lawes and conditions ... For be ye sure that I have placed you in this seate upon this condition' (Bentley, 309).

A typical tactic was to shelter behind the higher clergy, on the grounds that the state of the church was their business, under Elizabeth's more remote supreme governorship. Thus, when it was decided, in January 1565, to take a stand against creeping nonconformity and to proceed with 'all expedition' against offenders, the opening shot in the war known as the vestiarian controversy in which puritanism first became an issue took the form of a royal letter to Matthew Parker, archbishop of Canterbury. The letter was drafted by Burghley, whom Parker thought to be the true initiator of the whole business, although its language was strengthened in the queen's own hand. Once Parker received his orders, he and his episcopal colleagues were on their own. When in March 1566 Parker printed and circulated a book of articles comprising the new standard of conformity, he failed to obtain royal endorsement and was obliged to publish it under the humiliating title of *Advertisements*. His correspondence at this time is full of complaints of the lack of political back-up. The *Advertisements* campaign was successful in stirring up anti-episcopal opinion, but not in solving the problem of nonconformity, which was indeed insoluble. Similarly, when the Commons in 1576 drew up a comprehensive list of complaints about ecclesiastical abuses and presented it in the form of a petition (which may have been a tactical mistake), Elizabeth, 'considering that reformation hereof is to be principally sought in the clergy, and namely in the bishops', referred their complaints to convocation (Neale, *Elizabeth I and her Parliaments, 1559–1581*, 350). Only occasionally, and under extreme provocation, was the queen persuaded of the need to confront religious dissidence head-on. The publication in 1572 of the seditious pamphlet, *An Admonition to the Parliament*, which saw puritanism enter its radical, presbyterian, phase, and the even more outrageous Marprelate tracts (1588–9) were met with royal proclamations—in the contents of which Elizabeth may, or may not, have taken a personal interest. As was apparent in the case of Stubbe, Elizabeth took particular exception to printed libels.

Elizabeth's contention with over-enthusiastic evangelical protestants was episodic rather than sustained. She reacted only when a nerve was touched, as in the 1570s, when she ordered the suppression of popular preaching rallies known as prophesyings, but it is possible that, had not Edmund Grindal chosen to make it an issue of conscience in 1576, nothing much would have happened. But since he did make it an issue, writing the most tactless, if courageous, letter Elizabeth ever received, refusing to obey her orders, Grindal's own career was destroyed and a major crisis in church and state was provoked. Noted patrons of puritans, including Leicester and Walsingham, recognized the need to avoid antagonizing the queen. The most public occasion for clashes over religion was in parliament. Some of these parliamentary movements for further reform were narrowly based, as in the drastic 'bill and book' presbyterianism of 1584–5 and 1586–7, others had strong support in both houses and sometimes, especially in 1567 and 1571, among the bishops too. Without exception, Elizabeth resisted every one of these initiatives but the 1584 parliament, where feelings reached fever pitch, found her on the defensive, maintaining that religion would be amended without the clamour of parliamentary debate, while commenting darkly about the need to depose bishops who failed to end ecclesiastical abuses. By such devices, she contrived to make her religious policy one of *semper eadem*. There were no reforms of substance, no 'further reformation'; so that James would later remark, in his own inimitable style, promising reforms on which he too was slow to deliver, that because a man had been sick of the pox for forty years that was no reason why he might not be cured.

72 Queen and council

There was an occasion, in 1583, when Mary, queen of Scots, chose to communicate with the privy council rather than Elizabeth, going over the queen's head or behind her back. She was told that Elizabeth was surprised that she should address herself to what Mary had called 'principall members of this Crowne', as if the queen were not absolute, and absolutely able to direct her own policy without conciliar assent. The queen held her privy councillors in high regard, but they were what they were by her choice, not birth, 'whose services are no longer to be used in that publike function then it shall please her Majestie to dispose of the same' (Lodge, 2.276–7).

That was constitutionally correct, and even politically realistic. On many occasions, policy initiatives favoured and even carefully constructed from within the privy council were countermanded from on high. In 1577 the English ambassador in the Low Countries, Davison, was told that Leicester was about to cross the North Sea with an expeditionary force. 'This is his full determination, but yet unknown unto her Highness, neither shall she be acquainted with it until she be fully resolved to send' (National Archives, SP 15/25/35). However, Elizabeth was not 'fully resolved', and no force was sent. In 1580 Walsingham reported that the privy council had decided to shore up a crumbling Scottish policy by dispatching 1000 troops to the borders. When the queen came to hear of the proposal 'she wolde none of ytt', and proceeded to cut the force by half. Later that day, Walsingham had to add a postscript. Elizabeth had had second thoughts. No troops would be sent. Walsingham, never an optimist, wrote that Scotland was therefore 'clene lost', and with it probably Ireland as well. 'My lords here have carefully and faithfully discharged their dueties in sekinge to staye this dangerous course, but God hath thought good to dispose other wyse of thinges, in whose handes the heartes of all princes are' (Hunt. L., MSS HA 1214, 13067). The Victorian historian James Anthony Froude emerged from reading the Elizabethan state papers to conclude that 'the great results of her reign were the fruits of a policy which was not her own, and which she starved and mutilated when energy and completeness were most needed' (Froude, 12.508). Walsingham, Leicester, Burghley himself, all had the experience of rustication from both court and privy council, when their policies and actions too obviously conflicted with the royal will. When the disgraced Grindal found himself *persona non grata*, he was advised on how to conduct himself by senior politicians who had themselves been in the same boat, or might be.

And yet no privy councillor was ever sacked, and offers of resignation were never accepted, Davison excepted. If the privy council was stuck with Elizabeth, Elizabeth seems to have been stuck with her privy council. She coped with a power relationship which was often troublesome and even threatening by distancing herself from the privy council, whose meetings she hardly ever attended. In 1578, as the Anjou marriage negotiations began to turn serious, Leicester was forced to complain: 'our conference with her Majesty about affairs is both seldom and slender' (*Relations politiques des Pays-Bas et de l'Angleterre*, 10.678). The result was that Mary was not the only one to deal with the privy council as if it were the government of the realm, or even an alternative government. Foreign ambassadors on many occasions headed straight for the privy council. In January 1576 Lord Talbot told his father, Shrewsbury: 'the Counsell be all at the Couert; they site [sit] daylie, and the imbassidors cum to them' (Lodge, 2.136). It must sometimes have seemed that there were two governments, not one, in Elizabethan England.

A number of factors intersected to enhance the role of the privy council in the Elizabethan polity. One was the idea of public service, on the Roman republican model, which all these politicians had imbibed as part of their education at the hands of classical humanists. This in itself meant that Elizabeth's servants were not only subjects. They were also, in their own estimation, citizens, and part of a society which was defined as a commonwealth, a term pregnant with semi-republican resonance. Their role was to moderate the defective arbitrariness of monarchy with the salutary, if sharp, medicine of counsel. Peter Wentworth told the Commons in 1576 in a speech (which he was not allowed to finish) quoting the book of Proverbs: 'for faithfull are the wounds of a lover, ... but the kisses of an enemy are deceitfull'. 'And I doubt not but that some of her Majesty's counsell have dealt plainly and faithfully with her Majestie' (Hartley, 1.428, 431). Classical republican convictions were reinforced by godly protestantism. To believe that the monarch was God's servant and instrument was to enhance monarchical authority. However, at the same time, it made that authority entirely conditional on God's approval, empty in so far as it was not exercised to godly ends, and all too many of Elizabeth's subjects, including some of her senior ministers, presumed to know what those ends were. This made Elizabeth's effective sovereignty dangerously dependent on a religious appraisal of her conduct, offered by preachers and other publicists, like Stubbe in his book *The Gaping Gulf.*

Above all, contingent circumstances strengthened the conciliar principle, and the public sphere, in Elizabethan affairs: the fact was that the monarch was a woman, unmarried, and without an heir of her own body, which left the succession a dangerously open question. In these circumstances, Burghley, a more radical thinker than he has sometimes been given credit for, envisaged a state of affairs in which the realm and its appointed leaders, the body politic, might have to take responsibility for its own preservation and perpetuation. That this was part of his political thinking is evident from as early as 1559, when he asked the Scottish lords of the congregation why they had not spoken and acted as a great council of the realm, a device often used by the commonwealth to correct errant governors. In 1563 he responded to Elizabeth's refusal to allow parliament to limit the succession by drawing up plans in the event of an interregnum for ongoing management of 'publick affayres' by the privy council, acting as 'a Counsell of estate' (National Archives, SP 12/28, fols. 68*r*–69*v*).

In winter 1584–5, with Elizabeth's life apparently under threat from Catholic assassins (especially in the wake of the assassination of William of Orange), Burghley and Walsingham, and no doubt Leicester, with how much knowledgeable input from the queen herself is uncertain, devised a bond of association. This intended summary execution for anyone threatening the queen's royal person, which clearly meant Mary. It was a document to which thousands of Elizabeth's subjects were sworn, attaching their signatures and seals, and if all their names were available it would provide the best and most inclusive listing of what is sometimes called 'the political nation', albeit for the most part a confessionally defined, protestant nation. While the ostensible intent of the bond was to defend the life of the queen, its deeper purpose was to provide for the security of the body politic in the aftermath of her death. Unsatisfactory as well as unprecedented, Burghley attempted to replace the bond with a new version of the plan of 1563: interregnal government by an enlarged conciliar body, now called *magnum consilium coronae Angliae*. This idea died the death when Elizabeth ensured that it would form no part of the Act for the Surety of the Queen's Most Royal Person. Burghley had proposed. Elizabeth disposed.

Wider involvements

The public sphere in Elizabethan England was broader than Elizabeth's relatively small privy council. Second-ranking servants of the state were evidently moved by the same public-spirited concern for the good of the body politic, conceived as a godly commonwealth. They too had internalized the Ciceronian principle that 'we are not born for ourselves alone, but our country claims a share of our being, and our friends a share' (Cicero, *De officiis*, i.7.22). Such were several of Elizabeth's diplomats, men like Davison, Thomas Randolph, and Walsingham's brother-in-law, Beale, as well as men not on the royal payroll but equally devoted to 'the public', like the London lawyer and 'parliament man', Thomas Norton. No one knew better than Beale how public business was to be communicated to the queen, even how she was to be handled. 'When her highnes is angrie or not well disposed trouble her not with anie matter which you desire to have done unles extreame necessitie urge it', and 'entertaine her with some relacion or speech whereat shee may take some pleasure' (Read, *Walsingham*, 1.423, 438). Many of these men, Beale above all, were intellectuals, sources of advice on technical matters, whether asked for or not. Such was John Dee, Elizabeth's 'magus', whose immense library, which she regularly visited, was a major intellectual resource. The queen was free to seek advice from anyone, not only from her sworn privy councillors, but no one, whether privy councillor or not, had the right, as distinct from the duty, to offer it. A quite contrary doctrine was prevalent in the political culture of Elizabethan England, and especially among some members of the Commons. They believed that the Commons was an extended council, where the privilege of free speech was no privilege at all but a duty to speak on matters of public policy, including those reserved by the queen to her prerogative; and not only for themselves but on behalf of those they represented, and even for that fiction, the entire nation. When Wentworth was examined by a parliamentary committee following his inflammatory speech of 8 February 1576, he declared himself to be 'no private person; I am a publicque and a councellor to the whole state in that place' (Hartley, 1.435).

This constitutional issue was at the heart of those (to be sure exceptional) episodes of confrontation between Elizabeth and bodies of opinion in the Commons, confrontations which had to do with marriage and the succession, religious policy, Mary. Neale believed that many of these clashes were inspired by a more or less militant puritanism, whereas his critic, Elton, reidentified this puritan choir as merely men-of-business, transacting affairs on behalf of their patrons in the Lords, privy council, and court. Elton was right to draw attention to the patronage links between such men as Norton and leading politicians, and to see in several parliamentary initiatives the displacement of issues which the queen had stonewalled in court and privy council, but wrong to play down the ideological intensity of the issues, and to have underestimated the capacity of these so-called men-of-business to be motivated by their own assessments of the needs of the commonwealth. Burghley perhaps put it best:

> I do hold and will alweis this course in such matters as I differ in opinion from hir Majesty as long as I may be allowed to gyve advise. I will not chang my opinion by affyrmyng the contrary, for that war to offend God to whom I am sworn

> first. But as a servant I will obey hir Majesty's commandment and no wise contrary the same, presuming that she, being Gods cheff minister heare, it shall be Gods will to have hir commandements obeyed, after that I have performed my dutye as a counsellor. (CUL, MS Ee.3.56, no. 85)

Or when he wrote 'our parts is to counsell, and also to obey the commaunder' (*State Papers and Letters of Sir Ralph Sadler*, 2.129).

7 Conflict with Spain

The death of Queen Jezebel

The conflict of policy and interest, with its considerable constitutional implications, was most dramatically demonstrated in the long-running saga of Mary, and especially in its dénouement in February 1587. The exclusion of Mary from the English throne was the lynchpin of Burghley's politics, and much desired by many. During the 1572 parliament, the bishops were particularly insistent that she should be executed, while in the Commons she was called 'the monstrous and huge dragon, and masse of the earth' and 'the most notorious whore in all the world' (Hartley, 1.312, 438). Mary was routinely identified with Jezebel, just as Elizabeth would become Jezebel in the eyes of Catholic Europe after Mary's execution. When Wentworth referred to Mary as Jezebel in his 1576 speech, he was told that she was a queen and that he ought to speak reverently of her, to which he replied: 'let him take her parte that list: I will speake the truth boldly' (ibid., 1.438).

Elizabeth's attitude to her cousin was naturally more ambivalent. She was well aware that Mary posed a constant threat, but no less aware of the risks involved in excluding her altogether from the complex equation of Scottish politics. Fundamentally, she was unreconciled to the dubious precedent of judging and executing an anointed sovereign prince, for whereas many contributors to the 1572 parliamentary debates regarded Mary as the former queen of Scots, legally and justly deposed (under the fiction of abdication) and therefore a private person, this was never Elizabeth's view. Perhaps deeper still was a justified fear for her own reputation, for if Mary were to die, international opinion would hold her accountable. Whether or not the bond of association was Elizabeth's idea, she would find it convenient to hide behind it, avoiding personal responsibility if Mary did have to die. At the time of the Throckmorton conspiracy in 1583, Elizabeth, in the opinion of Walsingham, overreacted in her angry denunciation of the French ambassador, Bertrand de Salignac de la Motte-Fénélon, who had been indirectly involved; and she was willing to throw the unfortunate double agent Dr William Parry to the wolves, perhaps to take the heat off Mary.

No such diversionary manoeuvres were possible in 1586, when the Babington conspiracy broke, with evidence of Mary's full collusion as clear as Walsingham and his code-master Thomas Phelippes could make it: a smoking gun. Under the terms of the 1584 Act for the Queen's Safety, Mary was now placed on trial before a special commission and found guilty, a sentence announced by proclamation on 4 December 1586. All that was now required was for Elizabeth to sign the death warrant. It would not be easy to obtain that signature. Three times in 1572 the queen had signed the warrant for Norfolk's execution, only three times to have second thoughts. This was why parliament was summoned, as Burghley wrote, 'to make the burden better borne and the world abroad better satisfied' (Neale, *Elizabeth I and her Parliaments, 1584–1601*, 104), but also to place pressure on Elizabeth, who distanced herself from its proceedings. At this point, another biblical phrase, and precedent, came into play: 'foolish pity'. When Mary's gaoler, Sir Amias Paulet, wrote 'others shall excuse their foolish pity as they may' (J. Morris, ed., *The Letter Books of Sir Amias Paulet*, 1874, 291), 'others' meant Elizabeth, and the reference was to the second book of Chronicles and the story of godly King Asa, who removed his idolatrous mother, Maachah, from the throne, but failed to kill her, despite Deuteronomy chapter 13, which forbade 'pity', glossed in the Geneva version as 'foolish pity', to spare even one's nearest and dearest, where idolatry was concerned.

The story of what happened next is one of the most familiar in all Elizabethan history, and yet its deeper constitutional implications have not always been explored. On 1 February 1587 Davison brought a sheaf of documents to Elizabeth for signing, including, somewhere in the pile, Mary's death warrant. According to Davison, the queen was fully aware of what she was signing, and sent him on his way to his boss, Walsingham, who was on sick leave, with a piece of black humour: she said 'the sight thereof would kill him outright' (N. H. Nicolas, 213). Davison was also to see that the warrant passed the great seal. Two days later, according to Davison, Elizabeth confirmed with an oath that the execution should be carried out, although he also said that it was his impression that she wanted nothing more to do with the matter, and favoured a hole-in-the-corner murder, which might have satisfied international opinion. However, according to Elizabeth, she signed the warrant only to be held in reserve against any new dangers and had not intended it to be dispatched to Fotheringhay Castle.

Davison, perhaps aware of the 1572 precedent, no sooner had the signed warrant in his hand than he took it to Burghley and

Sir Thomas Bromley, lord chancellor, who attached the great seal at 5 o'clock on the afternoon of 1 February. On 3 February Burghley convened the entire privy council to meet in his private chamber at court, and secured their signatures to the commission under which the warrant was executed, Walsingham adding his from his sickbed. The documents were then taken to Fotheringhay by Beale's servant, George Digby. Mary was executed on 8 February.

There followed a storm which drove Burghley out of court and parliament for weeks. Camden wrote that Elizabeth conceived 'or pretended' great grief, and anger against Davison in particular, but then he thought better of 'pretended' and removed it from an intended second edition of his *Annales* (*Camdeni annales*, ed. Hearne, 2.546). If her strategy was to exonerate herself by shifting the blame on to her privy councillors, the self-preserving concern of those privy councillors, Burghley above all, was to make Davison the scapegoat. At his trial in the court of Star Chamber, the nub of the matter was Davison's word against the queen's (whether or not she told him to delay the matter), and against Burghley's (whether or not he had told Burghley that he could safely go ahead). In these circumstances it was inevitable that Davison should be found guilty, imprisoned in the Tower and fined 10,000 marks (a sentence later remitted). What is remarkable about the trial is that almost all the speeches were favourable to Davison, and the extraordinary procedure which Burghley and the privy council had followed. Arthur Grey, fourteenth Baron Grey of Wilton, thought it was Davison's simple duty to reveal such weighty matters to the privy council, 'whom it specially concerned to know' (BL, Add. MS 48027, fol. 675*r*), implying that the privy council also acted properly, in the interest of the safety of the realm. Only John Lumley, Baron Lumley, took up what was surely a constitutionally more correct position. It was a contempt, *lèse-majesté*, for the privy council to have met in the queen's very house, and to have resolved a matter of such consequence without her advice, or even knowledge.

Almost the last word was left to Richard Fletcher, the dean of Peterborough, who officiated on the scaffold at Fotheringhay, and who broke the stunned silence as Mary's head fell from her shoulders with the ringing cry: 'so perish all the queen's enemies!' His 'Sermon preached before the queene immediately after the execucion of the queene of Scottes', was remarkable both for its rhetorical dexterity and for its courage. He was not afraid to compare Elizabeth with the disciples, who slept while Christ prayed and groaned in the Garden of Gethsemane, which was to apply, and more directly, the trope of the negligent prince which is found in Sidney's *Arcadia* (Walker, 122–3).

Crisis in the Netherlands

England was in a state of semi-war with Spain from the late 1570s. It was also a privatized war. There was 'no peace beyond the line', where maritime operations, conducted by licensed pirates, technically 'privateers', of whom Francis Drake was only the most celebrated, preyed upon Spanish shipping and treasure. Drake's impudent circumnavigation of the world, between 1577 and 1580, defied its division between the Iberian powers under the treaty of Tordesillas of 1494. This was a venture in which Elizabeth invested, and to some advantage, and she rewarded Drake with a knighthood when he returned to the Thames with his booty. Drake's exploits decided Philip in favour of the Armada, defence of his empire by means of a single strike. This was easier said than done. Philip's experts calculated that a fleet would be needed larger than that at

Lepanto in 1571, and in 1585 there were no cannon balls available in Spain.

For the time being there was no declaration of war, and no commitment of English forces to the Low Countries, the cockpit of Europe since 1567. Leicester's hopes of a command in that theatre were dashed in 1577, but many English volunteers were active in a conflict which galvanized the aspirations of those who increasingly understood European politics in confessional terms as a universal religious war, among them Sir Philip Sidney. In the early 1580s events and circumstances drove Elizabeth inexorably towards the conflict which she had been so anxious to avoid. Anjou, for what he was worth, died in 1584, his brother, now Henri III, having proved unwilling to support his intervention in the Low Countries. Spain was now better placed to make trouble in France than France was in the Low Countries. William of Orange, the only credible national Dutch leader, was assassinated on 1 July 1584. Most menacing of all developments, in 1580 the Portuguese succession fell into Philip's lap, uniting two world empires, and two fleets. Now Spain, given time, could hope to deploy in Atlantic waters a fleet capable of taking on the Elizabethan navy, which made the 'Enterprise of England' no longer a pipe dream but a realizable project. If Philip were to regain undisputed control of his Dutch possessions, and Alessandro Farnese, prince of Parma, looked likely to achieve just that, it was hard to see what could save England.

By the end of 1584 the privy council accepted the need to intervene directly in the Low Countries, and in 1585 England entered into treaty obligations with the Dutch rebels. When Spain seized English shipping in Spanish harbours this was an added provocation, alienating English merchants who had been in favour of maintaining normal trading relations with the Iberian peninsula. So began a state of hostilities which was ended only in 1604, one of the longest-running wars in English history. Between 1585 and 1604 about 106,000 men out of a population of four million were conscripted for military service. The wars cost the crown £4,500,000, when its ordinary revenue was £300,000 a year. This was also the first major ideological war in English history, since the combatants, in the perception and rhetoric of the time, represented the forces of light and darkness, Christ and Antichrist. Also, it was a war with global economic consequences, as English trade began to redeploy from traditional continental markets into the wider world.

Throughout these years there was no declaration of war from either side, and for Elizabeth nothing was that simple or decisive. In her assessment of what might and should be attempted, numbers counted for more than ideology. She doubted whether she could afford the destiny which history now offered, and even after the treaty of Nonsuch with the Dutch was signed in August 1585, she tried to limit her commitment. She had no imperial ambitions, in fact some would say no ambitions at all beyond going on being queen, and in making limited war she was still seeking peace. So Elizabeth told Leicester: 'we do require you that you rather bend your cause to make a defensive than offensive war, and that you seek by all the means you may to avoid the hazard of a battle' (Haigh, *Elizabeth I*, 130).

The treaty of Nonsuch translated into an annual outlay of £126,180 10*s*., or a third of the ordinary expenditure of government. Elizabeth's reputation for penny-pinching parsimony, which largely derives from the Dutch adventure, is not really justified. Like other government initiatives in more recent history, the project outran its pre-estimated costs, but the queen was unwilling to foot the extra bill, or to accept that she had made an open-ended commitment. Under their treaty obligations, it was up to the Dutch to meet the shortfall. In the event, Leicester's expeditionary force of 7000, officered by his friends, many of them puritans, failed to cover itself with glory, a failure partially redeemed, in true English style, by the affecting death of Sidney on 17 October 1586.

The intervention also proved a political fiasco, when Leicester, flattered by his welcome, accepted the office of governor-general in February 1586, which implied that Elizabeth was sovereign of the Netherlands and he her viceroy. The queen let it be known:

> how highly upon just cause we are offended with his last late acceptation of the government of those provinces, being done contrary to our commandment . . . which we do repute to be a very great and strange contempt least looked for at his hands, being he is a creature of our own. (*Collected Works*, 269)

Elizabeth knew not only that she was being bounced, but that the world would assume that Leicester was following her secret orders, contrary to the war aims published in her *A Declaration of the Causes Mooving the Queene to Give Aide to the Oppressed in the Lowe Countries* (English, Latin, Dutch, and Italian editions). Leicester was commanded to resign his governorship, on pain of his allegiance—which he failed to do. Elizabeth wrote to Sir Thomas Heneage in the Netherlands: 'Jesus, what availeth wit when it fails the owner at greatest need! Do what you are bidden' (ibid., 280). Leicester was recalled in November, later given a second chance, but again recalled in November 1587, frustrated and defeated not so much by Parma, who was now keeping his powder dry against the expected arrival of the Armada, as by the complexities of Dutch politics.

The defeat of the Armada

Meanwhile, Drake, John Hawkins, and other privateers continued, with varying success, to prey upon Spanish shipping, coasts, and islands, a policy in the estimation of many more profitable, literally, than siege warfare in the Low Countries. In 1587, in the operation known to schoolboy history as the 'singeing of the king of Spaines beard', Drake destroyed much enemy shipping at Cadiz, together with the barrel staves intended for the Armada's water casks, so delaying the enterprise by a year; and he returned from the Azores with a booty of £140,000, of which Elizabeth, as the major investor, pocketed the lion's share, £40,000 (F. Bacon, *Considerations Touching a Warre with Spaine*, 1629, 40). However, it was beyond English naval capacity to maintain a permanent blockade of the Iberian ports, and if the Armada was coming, the fleet would be needed in home waters. On 30 May 1588, 130 ships, carrying over 18,000 men, set sail from Lisbon. The purpose of this supposedly 'invincible' Armada was to form an escort for the main invasion force, Parma's army. Harassed along the length of the English Channel by small squadrons commanded by Charles Howard, second Baron Howard of Effingham, Drake, Hawkins, and Martin Frobisher, the Armada reached the roads of Calais on 6 August.

Elizabeth prepared to receive the Armada with more efforts to advance the peace process in the Low Countries, negotiations doomed to failure but which were still in progress when the Spanish ships appeared in the channel. The myth that the might of Spain was overcome by England's little ships is far from the true story. The English fleet was in fact the most up-to-date and formidably armed in existence. The odds were stacked against England only if the Armada succeeded in landing Parma's expeditionary force. Yet, the logistics of co-ordinating the ships of Don Alonso Pérez de Guzmán el Bueno, seventh duke of Medina Sidonia, with Parma's soldiers proved extremely problematic. With little or no prospect of success for the combined operation which was the whole point of the exercise, the advantage was seized by the English fleet on 7 August through the use of eight fireships, the existence of which was successfully hidden from the Spanish. It was a small but decisive victory, assisted by the weather. As the Spanish fleet, still more or less intact with some 112 vessels, was driven northwards, around Scotland to a series of shipwrecks in the Atlantic and on Irish coasts, Elizabeth struck the Armada medal which sounded a note of protestant providentialism rather than triumphalism. 'God breathed and they were scattered.' Sixty ships made it home to Spain, but 15,000 men perished. Henry Kamen, Philip's biographer, found little to be said in defence of the enterprise of England: 'Neither the king nor anyone else was quite sure what it was meant to achieve' (Kamen, 276).

Elizabeth paid her famous visit to the hastily assembled camp on the north side of the Thames estuary, at west Tilbury, on 8 August. Garrett Mattingly offered two alternative visions of the queen inspecting her troops, escorted by Leicester: a majestic figure clothed in white velvet on a white steed, the sun shining off her silver breastplate; or:

> a battered, rather scraggy spinster in her middle fifties perched on a fat white horse, her teeth black, her red wig slightly askew, dangling a toy sword and wearing an absurd

> little piece of parade-armour like something out of a theatrical property-box. (Mattingly, 195)

However, the speech which Elizabeth made the next day was pure magic. Although it exists only in versions of what was transmitted and recorded by the chaplain Lionel Sharp, who claimed 'no man hath it but myself, and such as I have given it to', there is no reason to doubt its authenticity:

> Let tyrants fear: I have so behaved myself that under God I have placed my chiefest strength and safeguard in the loyal hearts and goodwill of my subjects . . . I know I have the body but of a weak and feeble woman, but I have the heart and stomach of a king and of a king of England too—and take foul scorn that Parma or any other prince of Europe should dare to invade the borders of my realm. (*Collected Works*, 325–6)

After this Elizabeth was persuaded to retreat to the safety of St James's Palace. On 29 August Leicester wrote to enquire after her health, 'the chiefest thing in this world' that he prayed for. After his death at Cornbury, Oxfordshire, on 4 September, she endorsed it 'his last letter' and kept it by her until her own death (Neale, *Queen Elizabeth*, 301). Warwick followed his brother to the grave on 20 February 1590, Walsingham on 6 April, and other core members of the old regime (but not Burghley) were soon part of history: Sir Walter Mildmay, Hatton, Knollys. A page was being turned, and Elizabeth, as she approached her seventh decade, stepped into a political climate so altered that it has been called her second reign.

Wars and the second reign

8

The cost of war

The year 1588 was by no means as decisive as a simplified and jingoistic history pretends. In 1589 Drake, as admiral, and Sir John Norreys, as military commander, headed a counter-attack. It was a complex, multi-purpose operation aimed at mopping up what was left of the Armada, attacking Lisbon, placing a pretender on the Portuguese throne, and intercepting the annual treasure fleet coming from the Indies, a kind of joint-stock enterprise in which Elizabeth sank as much as £60,000. The strategy was no better than that of Spain in 1588, and the result was a smaller-scale mirror image of the Spanish failure. In the summers which followed there were more naval ventures, concerned as much with profit as with winning a war. The lonely stand of Sir Richard Grenville and the *Revenge* on 2 September 1591 contributed to England's naval mythology, while in 1592 the queen's ships captured the great carrack *Madre di Dios*, a return of £80,000 on an investment of £3000. New Spanish armadas were sent to the waters around Britain and Ireland in 1596, 1597, and 1601.

The dagger still pointed at Elizabeth's heart was Parma and his army in the Low Countries. The emphasis now shifted to France, where the assassination in July 1589 of the last of the Valois, Henri III, saw the legitimate succession pass to the Bourbon and protestant king of Navarre as Henri IV, whose claims were contested by the remnants of the Guise faction, and by Parma, backed up by the popular politics of the Catholic league, entrenched in Paris. If Spain was not to dominate western Europe, from the Strait of Gibraltar to Friesland, England would have to engage Spanish power in France. The theatre of engagement was Normandy under the command of Sir Roger Williams and later Robert Devereux, second earl of Essex, and Brittany under Norreys. The first objective was Rouen, and beyond that, control of Paris, which Henri IV gained in 1593, not so much by conquest as by conversion to Catholicism. Elizabeth's response to this event was typically convoluted:

> And where you promise me all friendship and fidelity, I confess I have clearly merited it, and I will not repent it, provided you do not change your Father. Otherwise I will be only a bastard sister, at least not your sister by the Father. (*Collected Works*, 370–71)

War between Henri and Spain was concluded in 1598 and the Dutch revolt entered its final stage as the United Provinces emerged as a viable state.

Elizabeth's correspondence in these years reverberates with impotent anger at the irresponsible conduct of admirals and generals, who were so often out of touch and out of control, the impulsive and unpredictable Essex above all. This was no doubt one reason, not to speak of its expense, why she disliked war so much. As with the Low Countries in 1585–7, she limited her involvement so far as she could. After 1594 England scaled down its continental engagements, to concentrate on a naval war which was supposed to pay for itself, but which repeatedly fell victim to divided counsels and objectives: Drake's and Hawkins's last voyage to the Spanish main in 1595–6, Essex's great Cadiz expedition of 1596, when strategic opportunity fell victim to privateering greed, with a repeat performance in the Islands voyage of 1597. Whether Elizabeth liked it or not, this expansive world of *Westward Ho*, ever popular with Elizabethan historians of a romantic disposition, tends to disguise the continuing importance of events on the mainland of western Europe, and, after 1598, in Ireland, where she was obliged to sink the bulk of her treasure and the proceeds of relatively punitive taxation, direct and indirect. English troops remained in the Low Countries until the end of the reign, costing about £1,500,000. The last five years were occupied with a process which one historian has called 'shuffling towards peace' (MacCaffrey, *War and Politics*, 220–25).

A regime in decline

By the later 1590s it had become a commonplace to speak of the 'halcyon' government of Elizabeth, but these were not halcyon years. Rather they were marked by war-weariness, high taxation, inflation, a succession of bad harvests, and recurrent plague. Real wages were at their lowest point in centuries, and there was a corresponding rise in crime and vagrancy. In reaction, a government fearful of religious, social, and political dissent and subversion became more autocratic. In 1591 the judges declared, in the context of a trial involving religious dissent, that the realm of England was 'an absolute empire and monarchy' (Guy, 11). The 'mixed polity', lauded by mid-Tudor publicists, which swung into political action in 1584–7, was giving way to an unqualified royal sovereignty.

At the same time the political system was becoming more corrupt and faction-ridden. A note survives that Burghley wanted burnt, which establishes that in the last two and a half years of his life, and in his capacity of master of the court of wards and liveries, he accepted sweeteners of £3301 when his salary was £133 a year, the crown gaining a mere £906 from these transactions. One victim of these processes was the consensuality in the protestant political nation which had characterized the 1570s and early 1580s, often, to be sure, induced by Elizabeth's own very different outlook on the issues of the day. There was a marked generational change. Those men of business, motivated by a high ideal of public service, who tended to die, if not poor, in modest circumstances, were succeeded by clever lawyers on the make, like Thomas Egerton, solicitor-general, attorney-general, lord keeper, and, eventually, lord chancellor; in his origins a Catholic and a bastard but who ended up as Baron Ellesmere and Viscount Brackley, his son and heir becoming an earl.

Elizabeth herself was part of this generational shift, markedly older and losing her grip. *Semper eadem* was now a principle of morbidity. She appointed no more privy councillors, allowing the membership of her privy council to fall to ten, and she failed to replenish her nobility. When she retired from the opening ceremonies of her last parliament, in 1601, it was noted that very few of the Commons said '"God save your Majestie" as they were wonte in all greate assemblyes', and that as she motioned with her hand to make room, one MP shouted 'yf yow would hange us wee can make noe more roume', which the queen 'seemed not to heare, thoughe she heaved upp her head and looked that waye towardes him that spake' (Hartley, 3.306). During Charles I's reign Godfrey Goodman, bishop of Gloucester, remembered that 'the people were very generally weary of an old woman's government' (J. Hurstfield, *Freedom, Corruption and Government in Elizabethan England*, 1973, 105).

Egerton said that he was 'unwilling to contend with competitors' (Hasler, *History of Parliament, Commons, 1558–1603*, 2.81). The 1590s were responsible for the Naunton-inspired legend that Elizabethan politics was dominated by factional competition. With the contest for office and other perks fiercer than ever, there was a new exclusivity in the operations of patronage. Historians have not always agreed on whether this was provoked by the Cecils, the apparently indestructible Burghley and his up-and-coming son and apprentice, Sir Robert Cecil, or by their opponents who increasingly clustered around Essex, complaining of a *regnum Cecilianum*. Either way, the Cecils were now telling their clients not to spoil their chances by relying on any other patrons, and Francis Bacon, for all that he was Burghley's nephew and Cecil's cousin, had to rely upon Essex as he made his uncertain way up the slippery political pole. It was a decade interpreted for those who lived through it in the light of the work of the Roman historian Tacitus, and expressed above all in Ben Jonson's play *Sejanus* (1603–4), itself a decidedly Tacitean drama.

Ireland: an insoluble problem?

Elizabeth was also queen of Ireland, although it was a foreign country which she never visited. Much of the island was 'beyond the pale'. It could be asked how interested she was in Ireland, and how well informed about it. Could she have located the Irish provinces, Leinster, Munster, Connaught, Ulster, on the map? Members of the Old English aristocracy spent long periods, voluntarily or involuntarily, in Elizabeth's presence, especially that great magnate Thomas Butler, tenth earl of Ormond (1531–1614), Black Tom, a remote cousin of the queen and a frequent visitor. So she would not have been short of Irish advice and intelligence, however biased by corkscrew Irish politics. She also met, from time to time, the Gaelic chieftains, including Shane O'Neill, whose world the Elizabethans made little attempt to understand.

Ireland was governed indirectly, through viceroys, including Sussex, Sir Henry Sidney, Sir John Perrot, and Sir William Fitzwilliam. These men were faced with the largely thankless and near impossible task of reconciling English common law with Gaelic Brehon law and English customs with Irish customs. However, distance from the court allowed the viceroys to pursue their own programmes, distorted by local politics and pressures from England. The options available for the reduction of Ireland to the English model of civility involved varying degrees of conciliation and coercion but these measures were resisted by the Gaelic Irish, and often by the Old English too, as destructive to their way of life.

Conciliation, especially the policy of composition adopted by Sidney from 1566, was not necessarily doomed to failure: witness the ambiguous career of Ormond, who was more trusted by Elizabeth's government than not. However, in adopting this policy the viceroys, Sidney especially, bit off more than they could chew, while the violent logic of events, and the thinking of most intellectuals who addressed Irish matters, led ever more inevitably towards the simpler solution of coercion, and, ultimately, conquest, the prolepsis of which was the brutal repression undertaken by Lord Grey from 1580 to 1582, in the aftermath of the Desmond rebellion. This was an atrocity given its prophetic chorus by the poet and Irish planter Edmund

Spenser in his *A Vewe of the Present State of Ireland* (written about 1596), essaying radical social engineering, not to say genocide; and poetically and ideologically justified in his *Faerie Queene*, 'an elaborate glorification of violence whenever this was employed to promote either civil or moral goals' (Canny, *Making Ireland British*, 23).

The forces working against English success included, above all, the failure of the Irish Reformation, which left Ireland irreconcilably Catholic and a dangerous hot spot in the war against Spain. Politically, the policies of successive viceroys only succeeded in alienating almost all native political interests, even in the English pale, where efforts to make the Irish pay for their own government had mostly negative consequences. Increasingly primitive ethnology, a thoroughly racist perception of the Irish as almost subhuman, encouraged a brutality no longer to be expected in England. The colonial option, 'plantations', was used to deal with Ireland in the hope that English colonization would instil English civility. The most ambitious of these projects was undertaken in Ulster between 1573 and 1576 by Walter Devereux, first earl of Essex, with Elizabeth herself an investor, but it was a spectacular failure. All these factors were conducive to the growth of a new kind of Irish national sentiment.

Elizabeth was not indifferent to the radically unstable Irish scene. She wrote to Sidney on 17 July 1577: 'you gave us hope to diminish our charges and increase our revenue, but we find the former still to be great and the latter ... is much decayed' (Brady, 152). As this suggests, her major concern was to limit the extent to which Ireland was a drain on royal revenue (how happy she would have been if Ireland had paid for its own government, as Sidney had promised). This was certainly a principal reason for the failure of successive viceregal initiatives. So far as Ireland was concerned, the legend of Elizabeth's parsimony was no legend, although the Irish government could not support itself from its own revenues, even in peacetime. More positively, the queen's instinctive conservatism was helpful. Her way was not to destroy her over-mighty Irish subjects but to balance one interest against another, and she put up with postures and gestures of insubordination which she would never have tolerated in, for example, the north of England, implying that she acknowledged that Ireland was another place, where they did things differently. In 1580 she told Grey, her latest and most ruthless lord deputy, that she had no intention to 'root out' the Irish, since she was 'interssed [interested] alike in our subjects of both those realms', carrying a 'like affection' to them both (Canny, *Making Ireland British*, 119).

Revolt and repression

Rebellion tended to simplify the Irish problem and to resolve the mind, but not necessarily Elizabeth's mind—she always took some convincing that her Irish subjects were rebels past redemption. In the 1560s Shane, with a valid but contested claim to the O'Neill lordship of Ulster and to the earldom of Tyrone, succeeded in making himself the queen's main Irish enemy, particularly by the threat he posed to the pale. He interrupted an intriguing career with a visit to the court in 1562, where the garb of his wild Irish followers and his rhetorical Gaelic created a sensation. Back in Ulster, he reverted to type. Successive viceroys, Sussex and Sidney, wasted four campaigning seasons in vain attempts even to locate him. Elizabeth wrote to Sidney: 'you are like to enter into so great errors for the government of that realm as are not to be suffered in one that is appointed to govern as you are'; while Sidney wrote to

Sir William Cecil: 'for God's sake, take me out of this world' (Brady, 233–4). Shane was killed in June 1567, by the very Scots whom English policy wanted to exclude from north-east Ireland, and this gave Sidney some shortlived relief. Other defiances followed, however, as one Irish magnate and his affinity after another declared, in effect, their unwillingness to behave according to the script written for them.

Ulster was the source of the much more serious crisis of the 1590s, the rebellion of Hugh O'Neill, second earl of Tyrone. Tyrone was a man of stature, ambition, and a kind of charisma, and he was treated with respect at court, and by the last reforming viceroy, Perrot. Yet, his resolve to establish an unchallenged power in Ulster led him into suspicious confederacies with other Gaelic leaders, and in particular with Hugh Roe O'Donnell of Tyrconnell, an old enemy who now became his son-in-law and military ally. Feelers were also put out to Spain, of which Tyrone made no secret. The Irish problem, never entirely insular, was now increasingly globalized, part of the war in which Elizabeth was engaged over large parts of the world. There was a steady drift towards organized hostilities, as the end of campaigning in Brittany released English soldiers and their commander, Norreys, for service in Ireland. In 1595 there were military setbacks, after which Tyrone was declared a traitor. However, still anxious to appease Tyrone, if possible, Elizabeth was more critical than ever of her representatives on the field and in Dublin, where second and third raters were now in charge. 'As is too apparent to the whole world there was never any realm was worse governed by all our ministers from the highest to the lowest' (*CSP Ire., July 1596–December 1597*, 266). The disastrous English defeat at the battle of the Yellow Ford on 14 August 1598 plunged most of Ireland into rebellion. Tyrone now openly expressed the doctrine of Ireland for the Gaelic,

Catholic, Irish. The English counter-claim, to be defending the true interests of the Irish people against their oppressive lords, rang hollow.

This was war in a more formal sense than Ireland had known, and Elizabeth was obliged to dispatch the largest army royal sent there by the Tudors, more than 17,000 troops. They fought against an enemy who was no wild Irish savage but a sophisticated and wily commander who put professional and disciplined troops into uniform. The inevitable choice to confront Tyrone was Robert Devereux, second earl of Essex, for better or worse Elizabeth's senior general, who was now sent (most reluctantly, for his part) to a posting which he knew very well would do him and his reputation no good. He arrived in Dublin and was sworn as lord lieutenant on 15 April 1599. As things transpired, Essex had a sense of the future as well as of the present parameters of the situation (the queen was sixty-five years old), and the role he chose to play was ambivalent. While Tyrone played hard to get in Ulster, Essex undertook what was little more than a militarized progress through Munster and Leinster. In fairness to him it must be said that the Irish privy council advised against an immediate attack on Tyrone, Elizabeth gave her specific assent to the Leinster expedition, and he was not given the shipping needed to undertake amphibious operations in Lough Foyle, an essential part of the strategy, nor the heavy draught horses required to move an army into Ulster. Essex's reaction to these setbacks was more than petulant. It was paranoid, and it was met by stinging rebukes from the queen. By the time Essex set out in search of Tyrone, little enough of his grand army was left. When he met his enemy on the River Lagan on 6 September, it was to conduct a secret parley on horseback, leading to a truce, which Elizabeth immediately repudiated as dishonourable. Essex reacted by leaving his post, against her orders, and, still booted and spurred, confronted Elizabeth at Nonsuch Palace, Surrey, at 10 o'clock on the morning of 28 September, while she was still in her night attire and without make-up—conduct which not only broke all the rules of political and courtly etiquette, but implied that in the earl's perception not the queen but Sir Robert Cecil, principal secretary, and his party were now in charge. If Ireland looked to be lost, the English state was in a scarcely more stable condition.

In Essex's absence, Tyrone proclaimed a virtually independent Irish nation, inclusive of Gaelic Irish and Old English, governed, under the pope, Clement VIII, by Irishmen, respecting only a nominal English sovereignty. Essex's replacement, Charles Blount, eighth Baron Mountjoy, arrived in Ireland and, between 1600 and 1602, achieved what his predecessor was either unwilling or unable to do. Ulster was stormed, while Mountjoy's lieutenants subdued Munster. In September 1601 the anticipated Spanish intervention happened, at Kinsale in co. Cork, and the Irish war turned upon a siege and a successful onslaught on that garrison. The Irish chiefs were now picked off piecemeal. The last to surrender was Tyrone himself, who submitted, on terms, a week after Elizabeth's death, still ignorant of that fact. Elizabeth died knowing that Ireland had been reconquered at the cost of its alienation, a price to be paid by her successors and for centuries after. The historian is left with the tantalizing proposition: Elizabeth's own approach to England's Irish problem, if not to Ireland's English problem, just might have had happier results. Yet the French ambassador, André Hurault de Maisse, no doubt reported faithfully, in the winter of 1597–8, that the queen 'would wish Ireland drowned in the sea' (*Journal*, 51).

The end of the reign

9

The aged queen

De Maisse arrived in England in late 1597 to treat with Elizabeth and her privy councillors about matters of peace and war. Only a month before, in October, there was a new national emergency when another Spanish Armada headed for Cornwall, only to be dispersed in an autumn storm. Once again, God had blown and his enemies had been scattered. Henri IV was preparing to negotiate peace with Spain (the treaty of Vervins, 2 May 1598), and the object of the de Maisse mission was to find out whether or not Elizabeth was inclined to join in the negotiations. The interests of the Dutch estates were part of the equation, Burghley reminding the ambassador that the war was 'a game for three persons' (*Journal*, 105). However, it appeared that the Cecils favoured peace, whereas Essex, the leading military patron, was all for continuing to prosecute the war. Calais was once again an issue, the Spanish having taken the town in 1596.

De Maisse's account of his mission was modelled on the 'relations' of the Venetian ambassadors, having himself served in Venice, and the record of his audiences with the ageing

Elizabeth are among the most vivid and frank of any pen portraits that there are of her. He found her face long, thin, 'and very aged', under 'a great reddish-coloured wig'; her teeth yellow with many of them missing, so that she could not be understood when she spoke quickly. Yet, the queen's tall figure was still graceful. 'So far as she may she keeps her dignity.' 'It is a strange thing to see how lively she is in body and mind and nimble in everything she does.' Evidently there was no sign of arthritis, but Elizabeth was restless and fidgety, 'for ever twisting and untwisting' her sleeves, and repeatedly opening the front of her robe down to her very navel, as if she were too hot. She fished for compliments, complaining that she was 'foolish and old'. 'See what it is to have to do with old women such as I am' (*Journal*, 25–6, 37, 58). A year later, in 1598, Elizabeth was no younger, when the German visitor Paul Hentzner described her oblong face, 'fair but wrinkled', her hooked nose and narrow lips, 'her hair... an auburn clouir [colour], but false' (Rye, 104).

De Maisse described Burghley in 1598 as 'very old and white' (*Journal*, 27), deaf as a post, and carried everywhere in a chair. Yet he was not allowed to retire, and in his last months he continued to attend the privy council and to take his place in parliament. His familiar letters to Cecil convey a sense of servitude, as he was forced again and again to undertake the journey from his house at Theobalds, Hertfordshire, to the court. (In 1591 Elizabeth addressed him, jocularly, as 'the eremite [hermit] of Theobalds' (*Letters*, ed. Harrison, 207–8).) He knew his queen, 'the lady', telling Cecil that 'she useth not to gyve audience in cloudy and fowle wether... but yet betwixt showers I do attend and follow hir trayne'. However, this was written to be shared with 'the lady', because he knew that it would amuse her (CUL, MS Ee.3.56, nos. 10, 14). In his final illness, with his appetite gone, Elizabeth herself sat by his bed and fed him with a spoon. The very last words from his pen, written in a quavery, arthritic hand, told his son: 'serve God by servyng of the Quene, for all other service is in dede bondage to the Devill' (ibid., no. 138). Burghley died on 4 August 1598 at Cecil House, Westminster. These affecting scenes and sentiments should not be allowed to disguise the fact that in the 1590s, after the deaths of almost all the other great Elizabethan politicians of his generation, he exercised unprecedented personal power, almost a monopoly, which he was prepared to employ ruthlessly to destroy a career like that of Perrot in Ireland; and that this hegemony was productive of destabilizing faction. Part of the problem was that the bond between Elizabeth and Burghley was so long-standing and so strong that she trusted him implicitly, favouring him above all others.

Court faction and the Essex conspiracy

De Maisse often referred to the factional politics of these years, the tension between the Cecils and Essex, sometimes indicating that it was past and over ('formerly there was always great jealousy between them in everything, one against the other... a thing notorious to all the Court'), sometimes that it was a present factor which was likely to determine the outcome of his mission. He reveals that it suited Elizabeth to live with a faction-ridden court, that Burghley found 'these Court broils' amusing, and that his son was 'altogether immersed in them' (*Journal*, 4, 18). These were acute observations. The competition between the Cecil and Essex interests was of a fluctuating nature, of necessity balanced by the need for co-operation (Burghley, Cecil, and Essex were privy councillors), and there were many episodes of reconciliation. Burghley seems to have been anxious to save Essex from himself, and wrote letters of encouragement and support when the earl set out for the Islands voyage in 1597, almost as if Essex was still the little boy who had grown up in his household. Yet this did not prevent the Cecil interest from taking advantage of the earl's absence to make Sir Robert Cecil chancellor of the duchy of Lancaster, and Howard of Effingham, earl of Nottingham, which Essex interpreted as a personal slight, a reflection on his service at Cadiz. It was a typical Cecil gesture to compensate Essex with the office of earl marshal, which restored him to precedence over Nottingham.

Competition there was, which is evidence of insecurity on both sides of the relationship. Cecil was forced to serve a long apprenticeship before being rewarded with the office of secretary of state, and when he was appointed, on 5 July 1596, it was intended to put Essex (who was absent in Cadiz) in his place. Essex found himself unable to advance his clients, Bacon most notoriously. Patronage and clientage became more exclusive, with ambitious men forced to make difficult decisions about where they were to look for advancement, and having made their hard choices, these clients tended to become so many tails wagging the dog of patronage. In the most unedifying of all Elizabethan political episodes, Cecil and Essex jostled to reap personal advantage at the expense of the other in the affair of Elizabeth's Portuguese doctor, Roderigo Lopez, exposed (perhaps falsely) as a Spanish agent who was plotting to poison her. Above all this was a quarrel of two extreme opposites: Essex the favourite, the soldier and would-be military hero, a man made for 'virtuous' action in the pattern set by his late stepfather, Leicester, and cousin Sidney, whose widow he had married, expansionist and European in his outlook; and the Cecils, consummate, and essentially insular, politicians. It was sword versus robe. Essex's fatal mistake, which he committed repeatedly, was to suppose that he could deploy his talents, his physicality and his popularity, to command an elderly woman with whom he professed to be in love, but for whom he seems to have had scant respect. Burghley, after nearly forty years of service, still wrote of the queen, even in his private letters to his son, obsequiously and as her bondsman, grateful for every sign of favour. Elizabeth's no less fatal error, the worst she ever made, was to suppose that she could control Essex and put him in harness with Cecil as she had harnessed Leicester and Burghley.

Although in the aftermath of his father's death Cecil contributed to Essex's downfall, and was certainly willing to kick him when he was down, the earl was the architect of his own nemesis. His reaction to disappointment had always been to sulk and to absent himself from court, a risky and counter-productive strategy. When in September 1599 he returned precipitately from his Irish command to shock Elizabeth in her own bedchamber, Essex was a desperate man, knowing that he faced political extinction. There was a real chance that he would use the Irish army to coerce the court and avoid that fate. Yet at first the queen treated the affair with relative leniency, merely committing Essex to house arrest under the care of a fellow privy councillor, Thomas Egerton, on 1 October. No doubt she knew that London was full of other returnees from the Irish wars, a by now disappointed and angry Essex following. Soon Elizabeth thought that she had good grounds for a charge of treason, and had to be dissuaded from putting Essex on trial in Star Chamber. Instead, a ritual submission was arranged, before a special commission of privy councillors and others, where the earl was censured and remanded in custody. Later in the year the sun shone again, as Essex tried to woo his way back into favour, but Elizabeth remained deeply suspicious. When one of her maids, the skittish Mary Fitton, invited her to join in the dance which ended a masque at a wedding, she asked what character Mary was playing. ' "Affection", she said. "Affection" said the queen, "Affection is false." Yet her Majestie rose and dawnced' (Newdegate, 35–6).

Affection was false. Essex was wading in a dangerous conspiracy which involved a plan to bring Mountjoy's army over from Ireland and some incriminating diplomacy with James in Scotland, whose English inheritance Essex promised to secure. The balance was finally tipped when Elizabeth failed to renew the customs farm on sweet wines on 22 September 1600, which was an important source of income for Essex and those who depended on him. The earl was now facing bankruptcy in more senses than one. Essex House was a cave of Adullam, full of desperate and disaffected men. The earl's popularity was orchestrated by preachers, and by the players who staged a revival of Shakespeare's all too topical *Richard II* at the Globe Theatre.

On Sunday 8 February 1601 came the dénouement, an almost farcical putsch. Summoned to appear before the privy council, Essex refused to go, and then took hostage four privy councillors, including Egerton who had come to Essex House to secure his person. With some two hundred followers, he marched on the city, declaring his loyalty to Elizabeth and announcing that there was a plot against his life. Cecil was only waiting for this, the way was blocked, and a herald appeared to denounce Essex as a traitor. By evening it was all over. Elizabeth proved as stalwart as at Tilbury in 1588, although there was some hysterical laughter. Secondary plots and rumours meant that Essex could not be spared, as Elizabeth had wanted to spare Norfolk, thirty years before. Within days he was found guilty of treason in a trial before his peers which he treated with haughty contempt, and on 25 February, at the age of thirty-four, he was executed, making a good end which was celebrated in a popular broadsheet ballad, *Essex's Last Good Night.* There was a public sense of ichabod. The glory had departed, and with it, according to Neale, the soul of Elizabethan England. Now there really was a *regnum Cecilianum.*

The golden speech

This was the twilight of Elizabeth's life and reign, but she had one final great performance to give, which she did, and to great effect, before her last parliament, which gathered on 27 October 1601. It was not a happy occasion, with the unhappiness crystallizing around the issue of monopoly patents on commodities, a value-added tax levied at the consumer's expense. Under the pressure of vigorous lobbying from soi-disant 'commonwealth men' outside the house, the question was, should the Commons proceed by bill or petition? Legislation would have limited the crown's prerogative, and the issue became constitutional, and heated. Then the queen, with perfect timing, gave way to all the Commons' demands. All injurious monopolies were to be revoked or suspended. The response of the Commons was a spontaneous demand that rather than receiving the thanks of a convenient number of MPs, the queen should receive them all. At such moments a parliament was pure theatre.

So the stage was set for the most celebrated of all Elizabeth's speeches, the so-called 'golden speech', which in more than one version had a life long after she was dead:

> To be a kinge and weare a crowne is a thinge moare glorious to them that see it then it is plesante to them that bear it. For my selfe, I was never so muche intized with the potent

> name of a kinge, or royall authoritie of a queene, as delited that God hath made mee his instrumente to maynetayne his truthe and glorie and this kingdom from dishonore, domage, tyranye, and opressione...And though you have hade, and maye have, many mightier and wiser princes sitting in this seate, yet you never had nor shall have anye that will love you bettere. (Hartley, 3.296–7)

Later ages supposed that this was Elizabeth's last parliamentary performance, but it was not. On the last day of her last parliament (19 December 1601) she delivered her last public speech to the realm, pulling out many of the same organ stops:

> My care was ever by proceddinge justlie and uprightlie to conserve my people's love, which I accounte a gifte of God not to be marshalled in the lowest part of my mynde, but written in the deepest of my hart

and, after a lengthy review of her foreign policy and conduct of the war:

> this testimony I would have you cary hence for the world to knowe: that your soverain is more carefull of your conservation then of hir self, and will daily crave of God that they that wish you best may never wishe in vaine. (ibid., 3.278–81)

Death

As Elizabeth approached her seventieth year she seemed in remarkably good health, still capable of riding as much as 10 miles on horseback, showing off to courtiers and ambassadors. However, in December 1602 her godson Sir John Harington came to court and reported to his wife a great change. Several contemporary accounts suggest that the death of Katherine

Howard, countess of Nottingham, on 24 February 1603 precipitated the queen's final decline. What a later English statesman would call 'the black dog' had always been Elizabeth's companion, and now it dragged her into a chronic melancholy. By March she was refusing food and unable to sleep, not even going to bed, leaning against a pile of cushions, not speaking much but fetching great sighs. In this condition she died a slow death, succumbing to bronchitis and, perhaps, pneumonia. The end came in the early hours of 24 March 1603 at Richmond Palace, Surrey, her last earthly dealings having been with her 'little black husband', Archbishop Whitgift.

The final depression was partly political, induced by the knowledge that all eyes were now on the succession. The long-running Elizabethan succession crisis had been reactivated in the 1590s, as the sands of time were seen to be running out. There were at least twelve people with some kind of claim. These included the Infanta Isabella, the favoured candidate of the Catholics who, as in Robert Persons's *A Conference about the Next Succession* (1594), found convenient arguments against succession by simple hereditary right. There was also Lady Arbella (or Arabella) Stuart, James VI's first cousin and granddaughter to Elizabeth Talbot, countess of Shrewsbury, whose great building projects at Hardwick in Derbyshire had aroused suspicion in the privy council. 'Thus you see,' wrote Thomas Wilson, 'this crown is not like to fall to the ground for want of heads that can wear it' (T. Wilson, 5). According to reports from the Venetian and French ambassadors (and Christophe de Harlay, comte de Beaumont, the French ambassador, was a confidante of Robert Cecil and particularly well-informed), Elizabeth in her last days, together with the council, was exceptionally concerned by the movements and activities of Lady Arbella, whose liaison with William Seymour, grandson of the Protector Edward Seymour, and son of Lady Catherine Grey, whom she would later marry, was already a matter of knowledge (BL, King's MSS 122 and 123, summarized in Birch, 11.506–8).

By 1603 few doubted that the prize would go to James, who had played his cards very carefully and whose path to the throne was smoothed by Cecil, taking over from Essex as his secret friend at the English court. Whether Elizabeth actually named James as her successor is the final conundrum in a reign full of riddles. The fullest and perhaps most reliable account of what transpired was composed by William Camden and Sir Robert Cotton. (Camden was at Richmond and corresponded with Cotton, who was elsewhere, but the relevant passage in the original manuscript of Camden's *Annales* is heavily worked over in Cotton's hand.) According to this source, Elizabeth, while still able to speak, declared that she would not be succeeded by some vile person (or 'rascal', an evident reference to the Grey line), and being asked what she meant, replied, a king, and who else but her cousin, the king of Scots? On the following day, according to a manuscript account in Cotton's hand (BL, MS Titus C.VII, fol. 57), she was already speechless, but able to confirm her earlier affirmation by holding her hands above her head 'in the manner of a Crowne'. De Beaumont's report is consistent with this. However, another eyewitness, Sir Robert Carey (1560–1639), confirmed only the hand signal, and alleged 'many false lies reported of the end and death of that good lady' (*Memoirs of Robert Carey*, 59–60). Carey took horse within minutes of Elizabeth's death to convey the news to Edinburgh, and there was general surprise and relief that the succession problem of 45 years standing was resolved so easily and peacefully.

Elizabeth's funeral procession, with lifelike effigy, proceeded to Westminster Abbey on 28 April. Initially, her resting place was a central position in the Chapel of Henry VII. But in 1606 James I moved her to the north side of the chapel, and erected a magnificent tomb close to her sister Mary Tudor. At the same time he brought his mother's body from Peterborough Cathedral and erected for Mary, queen of Scots a tomb twice the size of Elizabeth's, and costing twice as much money.

The image and the memory of Elizabeth

10

Representations, allegories, and images

In this account of Elizabeth's life, the dichotomy of woman and queen has been constantly emphasized; but actually there is a trichotomy, the third facet being that of image and allegory. Elizabeth played many parts and enjoyed a range of mythical, symbolical, and metaphorical existences. This Elizabethan world of infinite contrivance is most familiar to readers of Spenser's *Faerie Queene*. His Elizabeth is Belphoebe and Gloriana: Belphoebe the type of virtuous and chaste beauty, Gloriana that of glorious sovereignty. Virtually every flattering female deity of classical and biblical mythology was pressed into service: from the Old Testament, the heroines, Judith and Deborah; from Greece and Rome and Renaissance Italy, Diana, Cynthia, and the Petrarchan mistress, the Platonically learned Laura. Most powerful of all these personae, replete with imperial and apocalyptic presumptions, was Virgo-Astraea, in Ovid the dying sunset of the golden age, in Virgil the promise of a golden age about to renew itself. On the magnificent engraved title-page of Christopher Saxton's *Atlas* (1579) Elizabeth sits as empress between the Pillars of Hercules, and in the portraits in the Armada series her hand rests on the globe.

Portraits of Elizabeth abound, the paintings grouped by art historians in a series of types or patterns. Sir Roy Strong counts eighty, together with another twenty-one group portraits in which Elizabeth appears, most famously in the so-called *Procession to Blackfriars* (Sherborne Castle), which has been connected to many particular and public events, such as the thanksgiving at St Paul's Cathedral for the defeat of the Armada, and to more than one wedding, although it may be simply a representation of the ageing queen on progress, carried in a litter. Strong also lists twenty-two miniature portraits, many of which were to be worn as jewellery—Elizabeth kept some of hers wrapped up. Most of these are by Nicholas Hilliard (or derive from him), who is unique among Elizabethan artists in describing the circumstances in which he painted the queen from the life, chatting while he worked about the differences between his technique and that of the Italians. (Hilliard also painted a miniature of Mary, queen of Scots.) There were also any number of representations of the queen in cameos, illuminated manuscript initials (with a particularly fine example in the foundation charter of Emmanuel College, Cambridge, of 1584), engravings, and woodcuts. Strong records thirty-two engravings and twenty-three woodcuts, but there were probably more.

In 1563 it was said that 'all sortes of subjectes and people both noble and meane' wished to procure the queen's portrait for exhibition in their houses (Strong, *Portraits*, 10). Portraits were also required for diplomatic use, especially at the time of marriage negotiations, but in 1567 Sussex told the regent of the Low Countries, Margaret of Parma, that 'the picture commonly made to be solde did nothing resemble' his mistress (ibid., 25). This sheds light on a draft proclamation of 1563 which attempted to establish, one supposes with limited success, a process for vetting and licensing images of the queen which would serve as patterns for the numerous copies which the public demanded.

Whereas most portraits of Mary, queen of Scots, are instantly recognizable, few of the many representations of Elizabeth can be described as likenesses. The exception to prove the rule is the fetching portrait of the teenage Elizabeth (Windsor Castle). However, as soon as Elizabeth became queen, many portraitists abandoned all naturalistic aspirations. Strong remarks: 'the whole structure of her face is inconsistent'—together with the colour of eyes and hair (Strong, *Portraits*, 17). A person has been transformed into an icon, an image of cosmic power and divinity, an object of worship, and, it has been said, less kindly, a clothes horse, since the great portraits are as much descriptive accounts of costume and jewellery as of the woman wearing them. The question of how many of the images derive from sessions in which the queen actually sat for her portraits is not known, although it is known that she was reluctant to sit, an aspect perhaps of her somewhat inverted vanity.

The coronation portrait (National Portrait Gallery, London) is accurate in its detail, including the loose flowing hair always worn by queens for the occasion, and it stands in a tradition which goes back to the coronation portrait of Richard II (Westminster Abbey). The formal and severe Barrington Park head-and-shoulders portraits of about 1563 may reflect the aftermath of Elizabeth's brush with death months earlier. In the Pelican–Phoenix portraits of the 1570s, which bear the mark of Hilliard, there is more emblematic and heraldic symbolism, the phoenix jewel of some versions representing self-renewal, the pelican in others mystical motherhood. The Darnley portrait of the same period (NPG) is one of the finest and, in terms of continental taste, most modish, although the identity of the artist is unknown. Strong suspects that Elizabeth did not sit for an official likeness again until about 1588, and the Armada portrait. If so, this would mean that the Sieve portraits, stuffed as they are with programmatic emblems and devices, were adaptations of earlier portraits. The best of these is by Quinten Metsys the younger and was discovered in 1895, rolled up in an attic in Siena, where it still hangs.

In about 1588 an industry sprang up producing copies of a portrait in celebration of the defeat of the Spanish Armada, the original of which was probably the work of the sergeant-painter, George Gower; ten copies are listed by Strong. The climax of Elizabethan portraiture was reached in about 1592, in the full-length Ditchley portrait (NPG) by Marcus Gheeraerts the younger, so-called because of its association with a royal visit to the house of Elizabeth's champion, Sir Henry Lee, in Oxfordshire. There is no doubt that the queen's feet rest on Oxfordshire, as depicted in Saxton's map. An accompanying sonnet deciphers the codes of the picture: the sun, surpassed in radiance by Elizabeth; thunder, an image of divine power; the boundless ocean into which pour 'rivers of thankes'. It is important to note that Lee, not the queen or any official department of royal propaganda, commissioned this portrait. Strong suggests that in the Ditchley portrait Gheeraerts ventured a realistic representation of the features of the ageing queen. If so, this ran counter to a late trend towards what has been called deliberate rejuvenation, well represented in the highly idealized and emblematically obscure Rainbow portrait (Hatfield House), which dates from the very last years. This is consistent with much literary evidence, with the tragicomedy of the Essex–Elizabeth relationship, and with the observations of the foreign observers, de Maisse and Hentzner, that while complaining of old age, Elizabeth did everything she could to disguise it.

Shaping a reputation

Several late Elizabethan observers reported that the English were tired of the reign of a woman and longed for a king. Experience of the rule of four successive Stuart monarchs overtook that prejudice and turned a legendary, not to say mythical, Elizabeth into a standard of staunchly protestant rectitude and militant patriotism, a stick with which to beat her successors and, ultimately, a whig queen. At the height of the exclusion crisis of 1679–81, a broadside proclaimed:

> A Tudor! A Tudor! We've had Stuarts enough,
> None ever reign'd like old Bess in her ruff.
> (J. Miller, *Popery and Politics in England, 1660–1688*, 1973, 74)

The myth of Elizabeth the protestant heroine was not created by the queen's earliest historians, either because they were cool in their protestantism, or because they understood the role of the 'politic' historian, on the Tacitean model, to be a dispassionate one. John Clapham, whose 'Certain observations concerning the life and reign of Queen Elizabeth' was written very soon after her death but never published, has very little to say about religion, beyond the same kind of denunciation of the puritans that is found in Camden. As Burghley's sometime servant, Clapham's book was as much a eulogy for his old master as for Elizabeth. This was one of several more or less abortive attempts to write the history of the reign. Bacon wrote no more than a couple of pages, and Sir John Hayward, whose historical interest was in alterations in government (such as the Norman conquest), covered only the first four years in his 'Annals of

Queen Elizabeth', which also remained unpublished and which conformed to the *politique* historiographical model.

Camden's *Annales* (1615, 1627; English translations 1625, 1629, 1630), more properly the result of his collaboration with Sir Robert Cotton, was an officially authorized and altogether more ambitious work, deeply researched and regarded as practically definitive for centuries. It owed its character to the circumstances of its gestation: first Burghley's commission, which opened the archives to Camden, and then the concern of James I that his mother should receive a better press than she was likely to receive from the great Jacques-Auguste de Thou, who had been over-reliant on George Buchanan's history of Scotland. Either because of his concern to placate James (a motive he denied), or because that was where his sympathies lay, Camden proved to be another loyal Cecilian (and Tacitean), who vilified Leicester together with his puritan friends, '*protestantes effervescentes*' (Collinson, 'One of us?', 156). He gave Mary a very fair press, with a longer and more appreciative obit than he accorded Elizabeth. It was Camden's translators, and especially Norton, who provided as it were fancy wrapping for this sober text and so helped to promote the myth of Good Queen Bess. To discover what Camden intended, as well as several interesting corrections and amendments for a second edition which never materialized, it is necessary to refer to the scholarly edition by the tory non-juror Thomas Hearne, *Guilielmi Camdeni Annales* (1717).

The eighteenth century qualified without demolishing the whig construction of Elizabeth. David Hume's *History of England* (1759) was for long the standard account of its subject. For all that he professed tory principles, Hume credited Elizabeth with vigour, constancy, magnanimity, penetration, vigilance, prudence. This was not very different from the version of Elizabeth found in the whig historians *par excellence*, Henry Hallam and Thomas Babington Macaulay (especially in his 'Burleigh' essay of 1832). For Macaulay, Elizabeth was more than a great woman. The whiggish, Victorian anatomy of her greatness lay in her identification with the nation and its destiny, her seemingly absolute power in reality dependent on the love and confidence of her subjects. This perception came to full fruition in the twentieth century in the work of A. F. Pollard and of his pupil, J. E. Neale. An altogether subtler variant on whiggish panegyrics is to be found in the great *History of England* by the Roman Catholic priest John Lingard (1819–30). As late as the mid-twentieth century, a good Catholic historian of the sixteenth century was held (by Neale) to be virtually an oxymoron, but Lingard has been called the English Ranke, the first historian to insist on the independence of history from both politics and literature, and he was a pioneer in basing his history scrupulously on the best, and often manuscript, sources. His research was at its deepest in his account of the Tudors. Here again is found an Elizabeth whose government was characterized by profound wisdom, although Lingard anticipated J. A. Froude in wondering how far it was *her* government, *her* wisdom. The hidden agenda lurking behind Lingard's scholarly impartiality was to disguise the normal prejudices of Catholic historiography in a book 'which Protestants will read' (E. Jones, *The English Nation: the Great Myth*, 1998, 175).

Revisionist tendencies

It was left to one of the great Victorians, the thoroughly protestant Froude, to burst the Elizabethan bubble, anticipating much twentieth-century revisionism. He created the modern study of the Tudors in his twelve volumes on the *History of England from the Fall of Wolsey to the Defeat of the Spanish Armada* (1856–70). He began with conventional admiration for what Alfred, Lord Tennyson, called 'the spacious times of great Elizabeth' ('A dream of fair women', l.7), but long before the end he had fallen out with the queen. He loathed her feminine tortuousness and artifice, to the extent that he came to share what he thought to be the privately held opinion of her privy councillors that 'she had no ability at all worth calling by the name' (Rowse, 'Queen Elizabeth', 638). Froude attributed all the achievements of the reign to Burghley, whose policies Elizabeth had done all she could to frustrate, starve, and mutilate. His Victorian vision of the Tudor age was a vision of emergent greatness, especially on the high seas, but it was a greatness achieved despite Elizabeth.

Towards the end of the century Mandell Creighton, for all his tut-tutting about Elizabeth's dubious morals, achieved a more just and balanced appreciation; which was odd, since he once wrote: 'as for the Tudors, they are awful: I really do not think that anyone ought to read the history of the sixteenth century' (L. Creighton, *Life and Letters of Mandell Creighton*, 2 vols., 1904, 1.288). He reversed Froude's harsh judgement:

> Elizabeth's imperishable claim to greatness lies in her instinctive sympathy with her people... There are many things in Elizabeth which we could have wished otherwise; but she saw what England might become, and nursed it into the knowledge of its power. (Creighton, 197, 199)

Creighton's respect is implied in the sumptuousness of his first edition, a leather-bound folio, embossed in gold. His account was spare and exacting in its scholarship, compared with the 790 pages of Agnes Strickland's fourth volume of her *Lives of the Queens of England* (1851), which was fulsome and marred by uncritical dependence on the Italian Gregorio Leti's *Historia o vero vita di Elizabetta, regina d'Inghilterra* (1692). Leti invented some of his sources and made things up. Elizabethan historiography in the Rankeian mould came to its dry-as-dust conclusion in Edward P. Cheyney's *A History of England from the Defeat of the Armada to the Death of Elizabeth* (1914–26), continuing and completing Froude's story. The biographical element in Cheyney is reduced to the barest minimum, with no observations on Elizabeth's character or achievements.

When in 1754 Thomas Birch published his *Memoirs of the Reign of Queen Elizabeth from the Year 1581 till her Death*, mainly based on the Bacon manuscripts in Lambeth Palace Library, he was critical of Camden, but suggested that the last thing that anyone wanted was a new history of Elizabeth:

> To relate over again the same series of transactions diversified only in the method and style, and with the addition of a few particular incidents, would be no very agreeable undertaking to the historian, and certainly of little use to the Reader. (Birch, 1.1–2)

Yet since 1890 there have been little short of a hundred books on Elizabeth of a broadly biographical character, not to speak of substantial histories of the period, like Wallace MacCaffrey's trilogy (1968–92), replacing Froude, and of aspects of the reign, such as Neale's two volumes on *Elizabeth I and her Parliaments* (1953–7), where the queen is given star billing, with all of her speeches quoted in full.

Most biographies have served a short-term purpose and can be mercifully forgotten. Neale's *Queen Elizabeth* (1934) has yet to be bettered, although it is to be regretted that his desire to reach a wide audience meant that there are no references.

He continued, indeed brought to an apotheosis, the laudatory tradition which has been persistent ever since the seventeenth century, as did A. L. Rowse in his *The England of Elizabeth* (1950), dedicated 'To the glorious memory of Elizabeth queen of England', and in his many other writings. In writing about the Sealion operation of 1940, which he compared to the Armada campaign, Rowse had coined the phrase 'the new Elizabethans'. The image contributed to the upsurge of interest in Elizabeth I at the accession of Elizabeth II in 1952, and the phrase itself provided the title for Philip Gibbs's book *The New Elizabethans*, published in the new queen's coronation year, which made direct comparisons between past and present achievements. Thus Drake's circumnavigation provided a model for the conquest of Everest by Sir Edmund Hillary and Tenzing Norgay, and for the test flights of Neville Duke. Gibbs looked back to Elizabeth I's reign as 'our flowering time of genius, high adventure, and national spirit', though he was less upbeat about British imperialism, which had begun under the first Elizabeth but seemed unlikely to outlast her namesake (Gibbs, 13). In the later twentieth century, a reactive revisionism began to gather strength: in Carolly Erickson's competent and spirited *The First Elizabeth* (1983), in a debunking collection of essays edited by J. M. Walker, called *Dissing Elizabeth: Negative Representations of Gloriana* (1998), and in another edited by Susan Doran and Thomas Freeman, called *The Myth of Elizabeth* (2003). The subject of Elizabeth has also been enthusiastically gendered, where, among much dross, Helen Hackett's *Virgin Mother, Maiden Queen* (1995) and A. N. McLaren's *Political Culture in the Reign of Elizabeth I* (1999) shine forth.

Fiction and moving pictures

There have been many fictions woven around Elizabeth's historical character but only one Elizabethan novel has achieved immortality, Sir Walter Scott's *Kenilworth* (1821). The novel is suffused with evocations of the period and many more Victorian readers will have learned a kind of Elizabethan history from Scott than from Strickland, Froude, or Creighton. However, although the book was widely researched, using available printed sources, Scott took artistic licence, played fast and loose with chronology. He conflated events, and invented some purely fictitious characters. *Kenilworth* is superficially about Elizabethan magnificence, but fundamentally about the falseness and venality that Scott discerned beneath the surface. Some passages, especially the account of the tragedy at Cumnor, read like a Gothic novel.

In the hills to the north of Los Angeles, towards Ventura, where the Hopalong Cassidy westerns were shot, there is an annual Renaissance Fayre which attracts tens of thousands of visitors. Among other attractions, an actress convincingly recreates Elizabeth, complete with tall red wig, conducted around the fairground by her courtiers attired in heavy furs, despite the scorching heat. This scene reflects not so much the historical Elizabeth as the Elizabeth of the screen, or rather the many Elizabeths, who have included Sarah Bernhardt, in a film of 1912, Lady Diana Cooper (1923), and Flora Robson cast against Laurence Olivier as Drake in Alexander Korda's *Fire over England* (1937). The Korda film was political, in the anti-fascist context of its time, and Robson's declamation of the Tilbury speech was so effective that it was recycled in wartime propaganda films. The film was denounced by Neale and F. J. C. Hearnshaw as 'second-rate melodrama' and grossly inaccurate, although these academic critics admired Robson's performance (Chapman, 17). In *The Sea Hawk*, a pro-British American film of 1940, Robson appeared as Elizabeth again, co-starring with Errol Flynn as a swashbuckling Elizabethan sea captain. Flynn was less at ease in perhaps the most famous of all Elizabethan films, *The Private Lives of Elizabeth and Essex* (1939), in which Bette Davis played Elizabeth, a role she repeated in *The Virgin Queen* (1955). In 1953 *Young Bess*, based on the Margaret Irwin novel, had Stewart Granger and his wife Jean Simmons re-enacting the scandalous Seymour story: a curious piece with which to celebrate the coronation of Elizabeth II. What all these films were about was the tension, even conflict, between Elizabeth I's private femininity and sexuality and her public, royal role, represented especially by her entrapment in the false little world of the court. How could Elizabeth resist Errol Flynn? Somehow or other she had to. Davis's Elizabeth complains: 'to be a queen is to be less than human'.

Glenda Jackson created the modern portrayal of Elizabeth in *Mary, Queen of Scots* (1971), in which Vanessa Redgrave played Mary, and then in the much-admired television series *Elizabeth R* (1971). In the 1980s and 1990s, any pretence of historical accuracy was gleefully abandoned in the TV series *Blackadder* and deliciously parodied in *Shakespeare in Love* (1998), for which Judi Dench won an Oscar for a few brief minutes on screen as Elizabeth. In the same year Shekhar Kapur won critical acclaim with his radically postmodernist *Elizabeth*, played by Cate Blanchett. As for the historians of the period, *Elizabeth* left them lost for words. It was as if the known facts of the reign, plus many hitherto unknown, were shaken up like pieces of a jigsaw and scattered on the table at random. However, with David Starkey's television series on Elizabeth, released in tandem with a two-part biography (2000), comes a return to what is perhaps more dubious: a set of images on the screen which can easily be mistaken for reality.

Reputation and reality

As the country braced itself to commemorate the fourth centenary of Elizabeth's death in 2003, her posthumous fame was never greater, Gloriana never so glorious. She was for ever on the television screens, thanks only in part to Starkey's skills as publicist and communicator. Publishers were commissioning any plausible author in sight to contribute yet another biography to the heap which already exists, confident that they would not lose their investment. It is not all that easy to explain why this should have been so. Asked why Elizabeth was great, the viewers of those programmes and the readers of those books would probably refer to her charm and affability. People would also have in mind great things that happened in Elizabeth's reign, as always, the defeat of the Armada, as ever, Shakespeare.

At the same time, professional historians have in many cases ceased to be dazzled. Paradoxically, this is one of those phases in Elizabeth's posthumous reputation when her personal stock has fallen in value. This is not because her political skills are unappreciated. On the contrary, an enriched sense of the texture of Elizabethan politics enjoyed by this generation of Elizabethan historians has if anything enhanced admiration of those skills. It is true that her instinctive reluctance to take decisive and creative action has never been so emphasized. Not even Froude called Elizabeth a do-nothing queen, which his successors have dared to do, but some biographers have decided that often it was the wisest course to do nothing, or to put off until tomorrow what need not be done today. Elizabeth has been praised not as the great achiever but as the consummate survivor, although others would say that that was not something that she could ever guarantee, and that throughout her long reign she gambled with the lives and fortunes of her subjects, above all through failing to make arrangements for their future government. However, a wave of revisionism in recent studies of the English revolution and civil wars of the mid-seventeenth century has meant that Elizabeth is no longer held culpably responsible for those in many ways calamitous events, which it is now fashionable to account for by short-term and contingent circumstances and happenings.

What has diminished Elizabeth's personal monarchy in the perception of the most recent and most academically minded of her historians is a growing realization of the limited extent to which it was in fact personal. The Elizabethan political culture was a complex organism, ceaselessly interactive at and between the many levels of society. That ancient formulation 'self-government at the king's command' proves to be a very true summary of how things were managed in England in the later sixteenth century. Elizabeth's subjects were also citizens of a commonwealth, ultra-conscious in the unstable and dangerous conditions of the time, the second phase of the Reformation, an age of religious wars and assassinations, that they were as much responsible for the safety of the state as their unmarried and heirless monarch. Elizabethan England was a monarchical republic; which is not to say that Sir Thomas Smith was wrong when he wrote in *De republica Anglorum* (1583) that his sovereign was far more absolute than any doge of Venice.

Sources

Primary Sources

Sir Robert Naunton, Fragmenta regalia, ed. E. Arber (1870) · J. Arnold, ed., *Queen Elizabeth's wardrobe unlock'd: the inventories of the wardrobe of robes prepared in July 1600* (1988) · [J. Aylmer], *An harborowe for faithfull and trewe subjectes* [1559] · T. Bentley, *The monument of matrones* (1582) · *John Stubbs's 'gaping gulf' with letters and other relevant documents*, ed. L. E. Berry (1968) · T. Birch, *Memoirs of the reign of Queen Elizabeth, from the year 1581 till her death, from the original papers of Anthony Bacon*, 2 vols. (1754) · *The poems of Queen Elizabeth I*, ed. L. Bradner (Providence, Rhode Island, 1964) · British Library, Lansdowne MSS · British Library, Add. MS 48027 · *Calendar of state papers: domestic series*, 1547–1603 · W. B. Turnbull and others, eds., *Calendar of state papers, foreign series* (1861–1950), 1553–95 · H. C. Hamilton and others, eds., *Calendar of the state papers relating to Ireland*, 24 vols., National Archives (1860–1910), *1558–1603* · M. A. S. Hume, ed., *Calendar of letters and state papers relating to English affairs, preserved principally in the archives of Simancas*, 4 vols., National Archives (1892–9) · CUL, MS Ee.3.56 · 'William Latymer's chronicklle of Anne Bulleyne', ed. M. Dowling, *Camden miscellany, XXX*, Camden Society, 4th ser., 39 (1990) · H. Ellis, ed., *Original letters illustrative of English history*, 2nd ser., 2–3 (1827); 3rd ser., 3 (1846) · T. Wilson, 'The state of England anno dom. 1600', ed. F. J. Fisher, *Camden miscellany, XVI*, Camden Society, 3rd ser., 52 (1936) · Folger, MS V.b.303, pp. 183–6 · J. Foxe, *Actes and monuments*, 4th edn, 2 vols. (1583) · H. Gee, *The Elizabethan prayer-book and ornaments* (1902) · J. M. Green, 'Queen Elizabeth I's Latin reply to the Polish ambassador', *Sixteenth-Century Journal*, 31 (2000), 987–1008 · *The works of Edmund Spenser*, ed. E. Greenlaw and others, 11 vols. (1932–57) · *Henry VIII, or, All is true, by William Shakespeare and John Fletcher*, ed. J. L. Halio, The Oxford Shakespeare (1999) · J. Harington, *Nugae antiquae*, 2 vols. (1769–75); 2nd edn in 3 vols., ed. H. Harington (1779) · *Letters of Queen Elizabeth*, ed. G. B. Harrison (1935) · *De Maisse: a journal*, ed. G. B. Harrison and R. A. Jones (1931) · T. E. Hartley, ed., *Proceedings in the parliaments of Elizabeth I*, 3 vols. (1981–95) · *Calendar of the manuscripts of the most hon. the marquis of Salisbury*, 24 vols., Historical Manuscripts Commission, 9 (1883–1976) · Hunt. L., MSS HA (Hastings MSS) · Baron Kervyn de Lettenhove [J. M. B. C. Kervyn de Lettenhove] and L. Gilliodts-van Severen, eds., *Relations politiques des Pays-Bas et de l'Angleterre sous le règne de Philippe II*, 11 vols. (Brussels, 1882–1900) · J. Knox, *The first blast of the trumpet against the monstruous regiment of women* (Geneva, 1558) · *Lettres, instructions et mémoires de Marie Stuart, reine d'Écosse*, ed. A. Labanoff, 7 vols. (1844) · Lambeth Palace London, MS 3197 · J. S. Brewer, J. Gairdner, and R. H. Brodie, eds., *Letters and papers, foreign and domestic, of the reign of Henry VIII*, 23 vols. in 38 (1862–1932); repr. (1965), vols. 6–21, *addenda* · E. Lodge, *Illustrations of British history*, 3 vols. (1791); 2nd edn (1838) · *Elizabeth I: collected works*, ed. L. S. Marcus, J. Mueller, and M. B. Rose (2000) · *The memoirs of Robert Carey*, ed. F. H. Mares (1972) · J. E. Neale, ed., 'Sir Nicholas Throckmorton's advice to Queen Elizabeth on her accession to the throne', *English Historical Review*, 65 (1950), 91–8 · J. Nichols, *The progresses and public processions of Queen Elizabeth*, new edn, 3 vols. (1823) · J. M. Osborn, ed., *The quenes maiesties passage through the citie of London to Westminster the day before her coronacion* (New Haven, 1960) · C. Pemberton, ed., *Queen Elizabeth's Englishings*, Early English Text Society, old ser., 113 (1899) · state papers domestic, Elizabeth I, National Archives, SP 12 · state papers domestic, addenda, National Archives, SP 15 · W. B. Rye, ed., *England as seen by foreigners in the days of Elizabeth and James I* (1865) · *The diary of John Manningham*, ed. R. P. Sorlien (Hanover, New Hampshire, 1976) · *The state papers and letters of Sir Ralph Sadler*, ed. A. Clifford, 2 vols. (1809) · L. J. Trinterud, ed., *Elizabethan puritanism* (1971) · R. Vaughan, *Most approved, and experienced waterworkes* (1610) · T. Wright, *Queen Elizabeth and her times*, 2 vols. (1838)

Secondary Sources

S. Adams, *Leicester and the court: essays on Elizabethan politics* (2002) · S. Alford, *The early Elizabethan polity: William Cecil and the British succession crisis, 1558–1569* (1998) · S. T. Bindoff and others, eds., *Elizabethan government and society: essays presented to Sir John Neale* (1961) · J. Bossy, *The English Catholic community, 1570–1850* (1975) · C. Brady, *The chief governors: the rise and fall of reform government in Tudor Ireland, 1536–1588* (1994) · S. Brigden, *New worlds, lost worlds: the rule of the Tudors, 1485–1603* (2000) · R. Bud, 'Penicillin and the new Elizabethans', *British Journal for the History of Science*, 31 (1998), 305–33 · W. Camden, *The historie of the most renowned and victorious princesse Elizabeth*, trans. R. N. [R. Norton] (1630) · N. P. Canny, *The Elizabethan conquest of Ireland: a pattern established, 1565–76* (1976) · N. P. Canny, *Making Ireland British, 1580–1650* (2001) · J. Chapman, 'Elizabeth in film', *Bulletin of the Society for Renaissance Studies*, 17 (1999) · E. P. Cheyney, *A history of England from the defeat of the Armada to the death of Elizabeth*, 2 vols. (1914–26) · P. Collinson, *The Elizabethan puritan movement* (1967) · P. Collinson, *Godly people: essays on English protestantism and puritanism* (1983) · P. Collinson, *Elizabethan essays* (1994) · P. Collinson, 'The Elizabethan exclusion crisis and the Elizabethan polity: the Raleigh Lecture 1993', *Proceedings of the British Academy*, 84 (1994) · P. Collinson, 'One of us? William Camden and the making of history', *Transactions of the Royal Historical Society*, 6th ser., 8 (1998), 139–63 · M. Creighton, *Queen Elizabeth* (1896) · S. Doran, *Monarchy and matrimony: the courtships of Elizabeth I* (1996) · S. Doran, 'Elizabeth I's religion: the evidence of her letters', *Journal of Ecclesiastical History*, 51 (2000), 699–720 · S. Doran and T. Freeman, eds., *The myth of Elizabeth* (2003) · G. Elton, *Studies in Tudor and Stuart politics and government*, 4 vols. (1974–92) · C. Erickson, *The first Elizabeth* (1983) · C. Falls, *Elizabeth's Irish wars* (1950) · J. A. Froude, *History of England*, 12 vols. (1856–70) · J. Guy, ed., *The reign of Elizabeth I: court and culture in the last decade* (1995) · H. Hackett,

Virgin mother, maiden queen: Elizabeth I and the cult of the Virgin Mary (1995) · C. Haigh, ed., *The reign of Elizabeth I* (1984) · C. Haigh, *Elizabeth I* (1988) · P. E. J. Hammer, *The polarization of Elizabethan politics: the political career of Robert Devereux, second earl of Essex, 1585–1597* (1999) · P. W. Hasler, ed., *The history of parliament: the House of Commons, 1558–1603*, 3 vols. (1981) · *Guilielmi Camdeni Annales rerum Anglicarum et Hibernicarum regnante Elizabetha*, ed. T. Hearnius [T. Hearne], 3 vols. (1717) · N. L. Jones, *Faith by statute: parliament and the settlement of religion, 1559* (1982) · H. Kamen, *Philip of Spain* (1997) · M. Levine, *The early Elizabethan succession question, 1558–1568* (Stanford, Conn., 1966) · W. T. MacCaffrey, *The shaping of the Elizabethan regime: Elizabethan politics, 1558–1572* (1968) · W. Camden, *The history of the most renowned and victorious Princess Elizabeth*, [new edn], ed. W. T. MacCaffrey (1970) · W. T. MacCaffrey, *Queen Elizabeth and the making of policy, 1572–1588* (1981) · W. T. MacCaffrey, *Elizabeth I: war and politics, 1588–1603* (1992) · W. MacCaffrey, *Elizabeth I* (1993) · W. MacCaffrey, 'The Newhaven expedition, 1562–1563', *Historical Journal*, 40 (1997), 1–21 · D. MacCulloch, *Tudor church militant: Edward VI and the protestant Reformation* (1999) · P. E. McCullough, *Sermons at court: politics and religion in Elizabethan and Jacobean preaching* (1998) [incl. CD-ROM] · A. N. McLaren, *Political culture in the reign of Elizabeth I: queen and commonwealth, 1558–1585* (1999) · G. Mattingly, *The defeat of the Spanish Armada* (1959) · N. Mears, *Queenship and political discourse in the Elizabethan realms* (2005) · J. E. Neale, *Queen Elizabeth* (1934) · J. E. Neale, *Elizabeth I and her parliaments, 1559–1581* (1953) · J. E. Neale, *Elizabeth I and her parliaments, 1584–1601* (1957) · J. E. Neale, *Elizabethan essays* (1958) · A. E. Newdegate, *Gossip from a muniment room* (1897) · N. H. Nicolas, *Life of William Davison* (1823) · H. Nicolas, *Memoirs of the life and times of Sir Christopher Hatton* (1847) · C. Read, *Mr Secretary Walsingham and the policy of Queen Elizabeth*, 3 vols. (1925) · C. Read, *Mr Secretary Cecil and Queen Elizabeth* (1955) · C. Read, *Lord Burghley and Queen Elizabeth* (1960) · A. L. Rowse, *The England of Elizabeth* (1950) · A. L. Rowse, 'Queen Elizabeth and the historians', *History Today*, 3 (1953), 630–41 · D. Starkey, *Elizabeth: apprenticeship* (2000) · R. C. Strong, *Portraits of Queen Elizabeth I* (1963) · R. C. Strong, *The cult of Elizabeth: Elizabethan portraiture and pageantry* (1977) · J. M. Walker, ed., *Dissing Elizabeth: negative representations of Gloriana* (1998) · K. M. Walker, 'Reading the tombs of Elizabeth I', *English Literary Renaissance*, 20 (1996), 510–30 · R. B. Wernham, *Before the Armada: the growth of English foreign policy, 1485–1588* (1966) · R. B. Wernham, *After the Armada: Elizabethan England and the struggle for western Europe, 1588–1595* (1984) · R. B. Wernham, *The return of the armadas: the last years of the Elizabethan war against Spain, 1595–1603* (1994) · L. Wiesener, *La jeunesse d'Elizabeth d'Angleterre* (Paris, 1878); C. M. Yonge, trans., *The early life of Elizabeth of England, 1533–1558*, 2 vols. (1879) · E. C. Wilson, *England's Eliza* (1966) · F. A. Yates, *Astraea: the imperial theme in the sixteenth century* (1975)

Index